**THE LANDS
OF THE
RAINBOW**

CENTRAL AMERICA

Photographs and texts
ALAIN CHENEVIÈRE

THE LANDS
OF THE
RAINBOW

CENTRAL AMERICA

Translated from the French by A.J.F. Millar

VILO
PUBL

Introduction

Central America is the smallest part of the continent first baptised America in 1507 when Waldseemüller, in his Cosmography, suggested naming the New World which Europe had just found after its supposed discoverer, Amerigo Vespucci. The slim Mesoamerican subcontinent links its two heavyweight neighbours, North America and South America. Covering an area of almost two and a half million square kilometres, it comprises eight countries: Mexico (1,953,000 km²), the former British Honduras, now Belize (23,000 km²), Guatemala (109,000 km²), Honduras (113,000 km²), El Salvador (21,000 km²), Nicaragua (130,000 km²), Costa Rica (51,000 km²) and Panama (75,000 km²). Geographers and geopoliticians disagree over whether Central America should include Mexico or whether it should begin with Guatemala. It is true that the landscapes and populations of Northern Mexico have more in common with the United States than with the other Mesoamerican nations but it is also generally admitted that the Yucatan peninsula cannot be dissociated from neighbouring Belize and Guatemala and that Eastern Panama lies like an outpost of the South American continent. Does this mean that we should draw some arbitrary border across the Mexican Oaxaca and another west of the Isthmus of Darien? Obviously not. We have thus chosen to define the limits of Central America as being those, recognized internationally, of the states involved: the US-Mexican border to the north and the Panamanian-Colombian frontier to the south.

This decision is supported by our examination of the ethnic and cultural identities of the eight countries in question. It is here that the first great American civilizations flourished, here that most of the descendants of the Amerindian peoples still live, here that the great and terrible adventure of the Conquest of the New World began and here, finally, that the hot blood of an entire continent simmers and seethes. A land of natural and human extremes, a cauldron of elements and ideas, Central America is one of the most fascinating places on this earth. From the burning deserts of some mythical Far West to the steaming tropical forests, from the snow-capped volcanoes to the idyllic beaches of the Pacific or Caribbean, it remains a land of darkly magnificent contrasts. It also tells us the story, often as dark, of its different populations whose culture and thinking have succeeded in bridging the past and the present without denying one or the other.

Central America is a land of flaming colours, of passionate songs, of revolutions and hurricanes... The pre-Columbian Indians thought that it was born of the arches of a rainbow sent down to earth by the gods.

Bordered by the three volcanoes of Atitlán, San Pedro and Toliman along its southern shores, Lake Atitlán, in Guatemala, itself fills the bed of a caldera or volcanic crater.

Bird's eye view of the Temples of the Cross in Palenque (Mexico).
These three sanctuaries were built by the Mayan sovereigns Pakal and Chan Balum, his son.

Summary

1
The improbable countries

The destiny of the Mesoamerican subcontinent is really quite extraordinary. Very small in relation to the Americas as a whole, it also appeared much later. It had no substance for Europeans until bold navigators, stubbornly convinced that there were lands beyond the "Great Western Sea", finally discovered them and thus began the conquest of the New World.

◁ *Now the symbol of Central America, the toucan, a brilliantly-coloured climbing bird,*
was considered by the ancient Amerindians as the son of the rainbow.

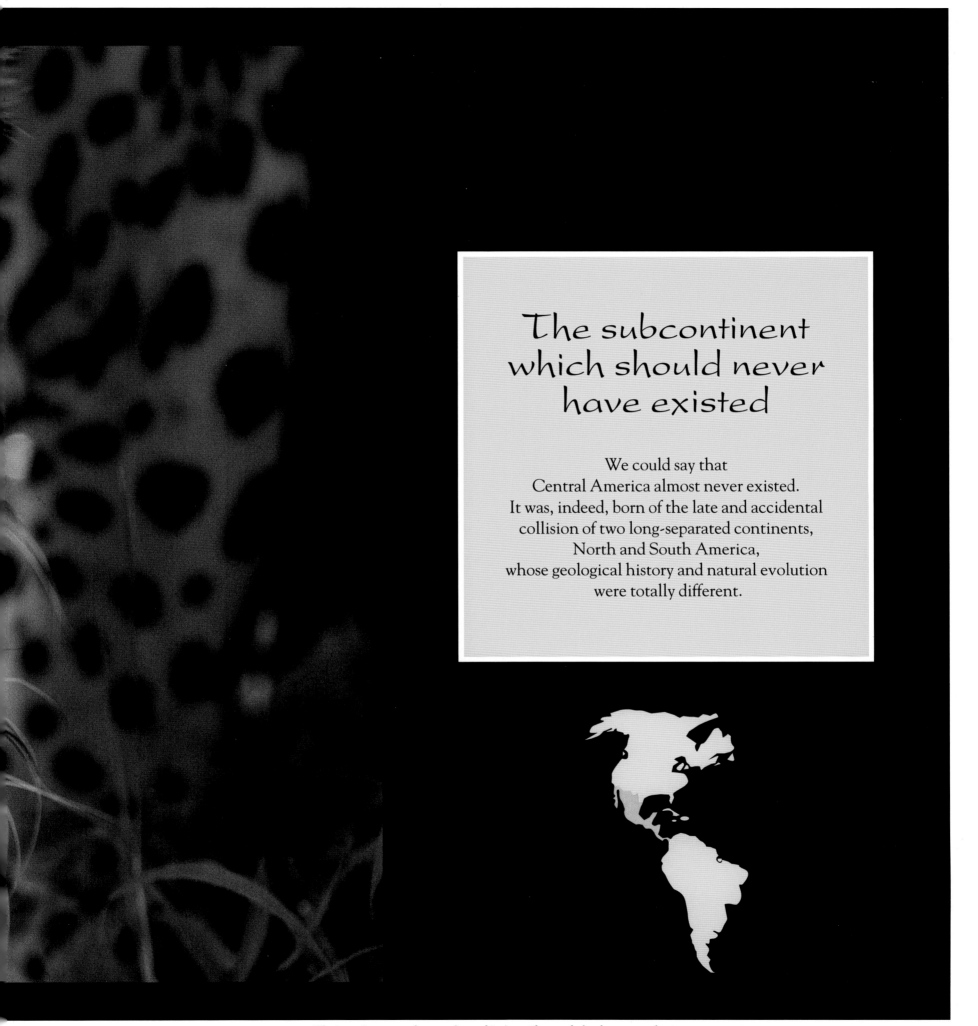

The subcontinent which should never have existed

We could say that
Central America almost never existed.
It was, indeed, born of the late and accidental
collision of two long-separated continents,
North and South America,
whose geological history and natural evolution
were totally different.

The jaguar's stare, so they say, freezes his prey with terror before he even touches it.
This magnificent panther was once common in the jungles of Central America but is now threatened with extinction.

Between two worlds

Around the middle of the Jurassic period, some 160 million years ago, a deep ocean trench opened between the two supercontinents which then made up the surface of the world, Laurasia in the north (comprising Eurasia and North America) and Gondwana in the south (including Africa, South America and the austral continental lands). Eurasia and Gondwana began to break up themselves into various continental plates during the following Cretaceous period. North America remained in contact with Eurasia through the Bering Strait, but South America broke away, completely free.

The plates began to drift and, some three million years ago, in the beginning of the Quaternary period, the two Americas ground up against one another. By then they had considerably diverged; the nearctic north

was composed of biomes ranging from tundra to deciduous forests whereas the neotropical south was quite the opposite, made up of deserts and tropical forests. Central America falls within the lush southern zone, sharing only very rare northern characteristics.

This complicated birth gave the Mesoamerican subcontinent three distinct geological identities; a northern part (comprising northern and central Mexico), a central or nuclear part (covering the Yucatan peninsula, Belize, the northern half of Guatemala, El Salvador, Honduras and the north of Nicaragua) and a southern or isthmian part (including south-western Nicaragua, Costa Rica and Panama) which is closely related to South America.

The north-American characteristics continue down into northern and central Mexico. The orogenic girdles of the Pacific rim are represented by Baja California, the Sierra Madre del Sur, the Oaxaca Sierra and the Sierra Madre du Chiapas. The Rocky Mountains of North America flatten and spread as they extend down into Mexico, forking into two high mountain chains, the western and eastern Sierra Madre, where several summits still reach 4 000 to 5 000 metres. The sierras frame a huge tableland, rarely exceeding 1 000 metres, in the shape of a rectangle lying northwest by southeast. These uplands are mostly composed of recently formed sedimentary rocks, covered with lava in many areas. Primary rocks and

Landscapes from the central mountains of Nicaragua, between Matagalpa and Jinotega.
Even during the dry season, when the rest of the land bleaches to straw tones, this fertile region keeps its verdant colours.

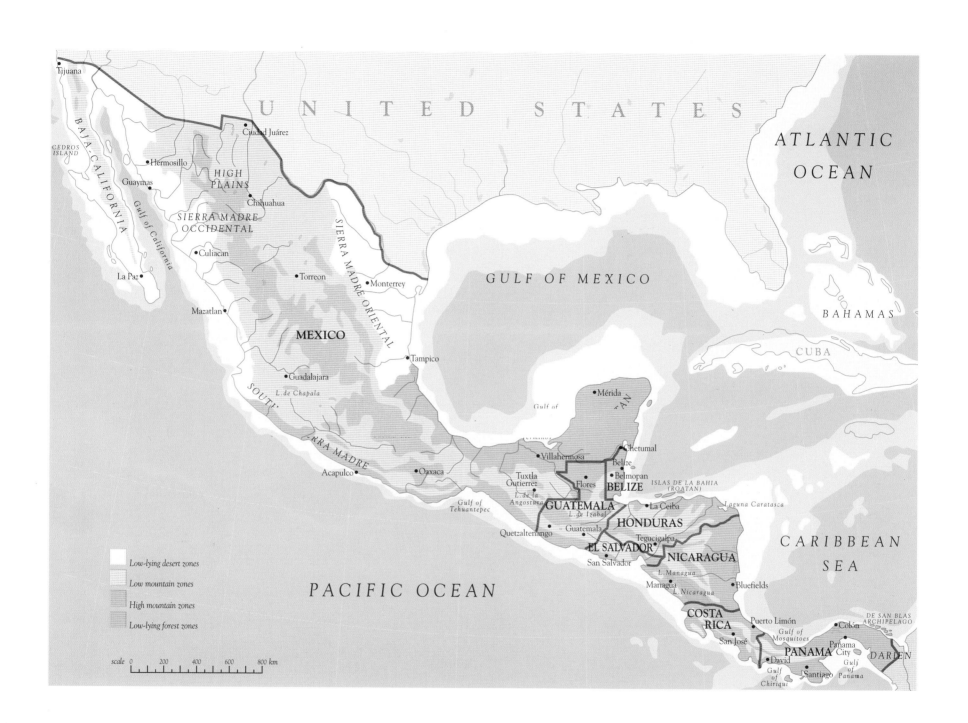

ATLANTIC
OCEAN

UNITED STATES

Tijuana

CEDROS
ISLAND

BAJA CALIFORNIA

Ciudad Juárez

Hermosillo

HIGH
PLAINS

Guaymas

SIERRA MADRE
OCCIDENTAL

Chihuahua

Gulf of California

Culiacan

La Paz

Torreon

Monterrey

SIERRA MADRE ORIENTAL

GULF OF MEXICO

BAHAMAS

Mazatlan

MEXICO

Tampico

CUBA

SOUTH

Guadalajara

L. de Chapala

Gulf of

Mérida

SIERRA MADRE

Chetumal

Villahermosa

Belize

Acapulco

Oaxaca

Tuxtla
Gutierrez

Flores

Belmopan

BELIZE

ISLAS DE LA BAHIA
(ROATAN)

L. de la
Angostura

GUATEMALA

La Ceiba

Laguna Caratasca

Gulf of
Tehuantepec

L. de Izabal

HONDURAS

CARIBBEAN
SEA

Quetzaltenango

Guatemala

Tegucigalpa

EL SALVADOR

NICARAGUA

San Salvador

	Low-lying desert zones
	Low mountain zones
	High mountain zones
	Low-lying forest zones

PACIFIC OCEAN

L. Managua

Managua

L. Nicaragua

Bluefields

COSTA
RICA

Puerto Limón

DE SAN BLAS
ARCHIPELAGO

Colón

Gulf of
Mosquitoes

San José

PANAMA

Panama
City

DARIEN

scale 0   200   400   600   800 km

David

Santiago

Gulf
of
Chiriqui

Gulf
of
Panama

intrusive granite outcrops appear on the mountain sides facing the Pacific. At the southern tip of the tableland, the mountains curve eastwards, coming together again to form a single range which rapidly sinks to the level of the Isthmus of Tehuantepec, the narrow neck of land, only 250 kilometres wide, separating the Atlantic from the Pacific. In geological terms, this is the end of North America.

With the exception of the Yucatan peninsula, northern Belize and Guatemalan Peten, mainly made up of sedimentary rocks (essentially limestone) which piled up on an ancient base during the Cretaceous and Tertiary periods, nuclear America is a sort of extension of southern Mexico. The Guatemalan mountain chains (the central ranges, the Altos de Cuchumatanes and southern ranges) are a natural continuation of the Mexican Chiapas structures. From eastern Guatemala, the central ranges are bordered on their Pacific

Two contrasting faces of Central America: the Bocas del Toro lagoons in Panama, fringed with the lush tropical vegetation of the Caribbean, and the desolate, cactus-studded wastes of Mexico's Sonora desert.

side by foothills which mostly appeared during the Quaternary and which are criss-crossed with other folds running northeast by southwest, pushed up during the great orogenetic upthrusts of the Tertiary and Quaternary periods. The mountains of El Salvador (Interior and Exterior Cordillera, separated by many massifs such as the Izalco, the San Salvador, the San Miguel and others), of Honduras (Cordillera Opalaca, Cordillera Nombre de Dios, Cordillera Entre Rios...) and of northern Nicaragua (Cordillera de Los Maribios, Cordillera Isabella, Cordillera Chontalena...), all more recently formed, are covered with many strata of volcanic rock layered over the same ancient base as that of neighbouring Guatemala.

Southern Central America is often called isthmic, a geographic term referring to the Isthmus of Panama, the narrowest point of the subcontinent (less than 50 kilometres wide at some places) and the bridge between the two 'great' Americas. As elsewhere, the most ancient elements here on the isthmus are composed of metamorphic and magmatic rocks, generally covered with sedimentary formations dating from the Cretaceous. A chain of relatively high mountains (many peaks exceed 3 200 metres) runs northwest to southeast through a series of countries, changing names as it progresses. Thus this mountain backbone is successively known as the Cordillera de Guanacaste, the Cordillera de Tilaran, the Cordillera Centrale in Costa Rica and the Cordillera de Talamanca, which continues down into Panama before becoming part of the great Cordillera Centrale. The other Panamanian uplands (the Cordillera de San Blas and the Serrania del Darien) are much more modest, barely exceeding 1 000 metres on average. Considered as foothills of the central Colombian cordillera, they are already part of South America.

Quetaltepec towers over the city of San Salvador (El Salvador). The volcano's twin summits, the Picacho (1 960 m) and the Boqueron (1 893 m),
and its graceful double crater are a favourite walk for the capital's inhabitants.

Like these great fissures at Madera, in the state of Chihuahua (Mexico),
land almost everywhere in Central America carries the imprint of intense seismic activity.

Capped with eternal snows, the two majestic volcanic cones of Popocatepetl (5 452 m) and Iztaccihuatl (5 286 m)
seal the valley of Mexico to the east. According to Aztec legend, they incarnate the mythical couple of the warrior Popo and his fiancée Itza,
who died of sorrow when her beloved left for the wars. On his return, Popo raised the two mountains in homage to her and has stood ever since,
in tribute to his love, waiting with a lit torch in his hand.

Mount Orizaba or Citlaltepetl, culminating at 5 700 m, is Mexico's crowning peak and the third highest in North America.
Despite difficulties of access, its magnificent landscapes attract many groups of hikers and climbers each weekend.

'Between two mountains' in the Nahuatl language, the island of Omotepe, in Nicaragua, ▷
is formed of a narrow strip of earth linked to two volcanoes, Concepcion and Madera.

The "cauldron of America"

The Mesoamerican subcontinent lies at the intersection of four continental plates (North America, the Caribbean, the Cocos Islands and South America) which grind against one another at speeds of 1 to 20 centimetres a year. The whole region is the seat of an intense telluric activity which never ceases, sometimes in shifts barely perceptible to humans, sometimes bubbling up in terrible catastrophes. Volcanic eruptions and earthquakes are so common that the region has come to be known as the 'cauldron of America'. Almost three hundred volcanoes line the edges of the converging plates. Many are extinct, but at least twenty show constant activity, located mostly in nuclear Mesoamerica, the crossroads between the North and South. The natural fertility of these volcanic soils is an obvious attraction for farmers and large populations live in the shadow of these giants, each settlement allaying its fear with some form of worship.

In Mexico, the best-known volcanoes are Popocatepetl (5 452 m), dormant since 1802 but giving off

occasional puffs of smoke and subject to a mini-eruption in 1996 which killed five people, and Ixtaccihuatl (5 286 m), both of which dominate the eastern side of the Mexico valley, Colima (4 265 m), Chichon (3 640 m), whose 1982 explosion left thousands dead, Malinche (4 450 m), Cofre de Perote (4 274 m) and especially Orizaba or Citlatepetl (5 700 m), inactive since 1687 and the highest mountain in Mexico. The volcano most famous for its activity is the 'little' Piricutin (2 774 m), also the country's youngest peak, pushed up in Michoacan in only 1943. During the first seven months of its existence, it threw up almost two hundred thousand million cubic metres of ash, scoria and lava!

The other countries of Central America have their own stars. Guatemala boasts Tacana (4 093 m), Tajumulco (4 220 m), Santa Maria (3 768 m), somnolent since 1902 but which abruptly awoke in 1996 before just as suddenly returning to sleep, Atitlan (3 537 m), Acatenango (3 976 m), the constantly active Fuego (3 765 m), Agua (3 766 m) and Pacaya (2 552 m), shaken by a series of eruptions between 1986 and 1996. In El Salvador, everyone knows Santa Ana (2 365 m), Izalco (2 385 m), dormant since 1963, San Vincente or Chichontepec (2 182 m) and San Miguel or Chaparrastique (2 130 m). Nicaragua fears the sudden rages of Cerro Negro (1 080 m), whose most recent eruptions were in 1974, 1992 and 1995, and of Masaya or Santiago (635 m), now again in activity since 1989. The country also features San Cristobal or Chinandega (1 745 m), Concepcion (1 610 m), Momotombo (1 280 m), which originally measured over 1 600 metres but whose summit was literally blown off by a violent explosion in 1905, Mombacho (1 345 m) and Telica (1 060 m), last in eruption in 1994... Costa Rica has its share of volcanoes, including Orosi (1 487 m), Miravalles (2 028 m), Arenal (1 633 m), in almost permanent activity since 1968 when it caused the death of 78 people, Poas (2 704 m), Barva (2 906 m), Turrialba (3 328 m) with its four craters side by side, Irazu (3 432 m), whose lava and ash covered San José and a major part of the central valley in 1963 and whose latest explosion was in 1992, and Rincon de la Vieja (1 895 m) which burst into activity on several occasions in 1983, 1991, 1993 and 1995. Panama has only one volcano, the dormant Baru which, at 3 475 m, is the highest peak in the country.

Another common feature of the earth's hot spots, earthquakes result from sudden landslips inside the Earth along the geological fault lines. Not a day passes without the recording of a tremor somewhere on the scale and major seisms, often accompanied by tsunamis or tidal waves, hit Central America at regular intervals. In the last three decades alone, the toll in human lives has been considerable. In 1972, Managua, the capital of

Nicaragua, already razed in 1931, was almost entirely destroyed again when an earthquake registering 6.2 on the Richter scale left 5 000 dead and over 150,000 injured. The following year, Oaxaca, in Mexico, was shaken by two earthquakes at a cost of 206 lives. A national tragedy struck Guatemala in 1976 when 22 868 perished in a major quake. Three powerful seisms in 1982, 1986 and 1987 took almost 2 000 lives in El Salvador. In 1985, Central Mexico was hit by a giant earthquake of magnitude 8.1, killing 35,000 people (including 5 000 in Mexico City), leaving 100,000 homeless and launching a tsunami over 8 metres high across the Pacific. Already shaken in 1983, Costa Rica and Panama were again struck in 1991 when 60 people lost their lives and 10,000 their homes. The Costa Rican and Nicaraguan earth trembled violently in 1992, taking some 10 victims and triggering an 8-metre tsunami across the Pacific. Other earthquakes shook Guatemala and Nicaragua again in 1995, leaving, as each time, a trail of death and destruction...

To complete this picture, we should also remember that Central America is often struck by tropical storms, hurricanes and cyclones. In 1973, the hurricane 'Fifi' claimed 8 200 lives in Honduras and the 1976 cyclone left 2 600 dead in Mexico. In 1995 alone, eleven cyclones and nineteen tempests scoured the Atlantic coasts, causing often severe damage in Latin America. The hurricane 'Pauline' took 200 victims in Mexico and, of course, the terrible 'Mitch' of 1998 killed over 20,000 according to official statistics, made 1,200,000 homeless and left behind it a trail of ruin and destruction, notably in Honduras and Nicaragua.

The symetrical cone of Momotombo rises north-west of Lake Managua in Nicaragua.
Its serene and reassuring appearance belies its terrible rages.

Again in Nicaragua, the volcano Masaya, near the town of the same name, is currently active.
It was considered one of the mouths of Hell both by the ancient Indians, who threw victims into its maw to appease the gods,
and by the Conquistadores, who set up the largest cross of the period to 'neutralise' the devil!

A couple of kinkajous. These animals are active during the night and early mornings, feeding on fruit, eggs, honey and insects.
They are now threatened by deforestation.

The land of extremes

Because of its position as a bridge between the land masses of North and South America, the Mesoamerican subcontinent features a wide range of reliefs and climates which, in turn, give rise to as many different types of vegetation and make it one of the most diversified regions in the world. The major part of northern Mexico is composed of a sweeping plateau, 2 000 kilometres long by over 500 kilometres wide, hemmed on either side by twin mountain ranges, the Western Sierra Madre and the Eastern Sierra Madre. On the low-lying stretches, the arid climate has led to the spread of deserts and steppe around

scattered oases where the relative humidity allows farmers to scratch a living. The two great deserts in these regions are the Sonora in the Northwest, shared with New Mexico, and the Chihuahua. Here the sparse vegetation is composed of many species of xerophyte grasses, which furnish meagre pastures for flocks, cactus, agave, thorn bushes and scrub. Up on the mesas, the ground-hugging scrub gradually gives way to dwarf bushes which are in turn replaced by forests of pine and fir on the sierras. These heights are the haunts of the wolf, the mountain lion and the deer. Along the western edge of the country, Baja California forms a dry, craggy peninsula, a finger of land 1 500 kilometres long and 110 wide, covered with desert in the north and down the middle. Although a western extension of the Sonoran Desert, its isolation has fostered a fauna and flora quite different from the rest of the country. These include, for example, over 800 species of cactus. The many land reptiles and mammals (squirrels, racoons, coyotes...) cohabit with the marine mammals like the grey whales, the sea lions and the elephant seals.

In the rest of Central America, the climatic zones are determined by height and morphology of the reliefs and by the prevailing winds. As a general rule, the regions facing north or northeast, swept by the trade cont. page 29

Characteristic landscape from the Barranca del Cobre mountains in Mexico.
This region, furrowed by deep canyons where rich copper deposits were once mined by the Indians and then by the Spanish colonists,
is now inhabited by peasant farmers who must wrest their land from the great conifer forests.

Mexico's Baja California peninsula forms a long, narrow sliver of arid land between the Pacific and the Gulf of California.
Its coast features magnificent unspoiled bays such as Concepcion, pictured here.

*Northern Mexico alone contains over 1 300 varieties of cactus,
almost 90% of the world's total population.*

*The island of Cedros and the San Benito archipelago (Mexico) are famed for the outstanding wealth of their marine fauna,
notably the mammals such as elephant seals and sea lions.*

winds, swelter in a very wet tropical climate which sustains luxuriant forests whereas those in the lee of the wind enjoy a drier tropical climate which encourages the growth of savannah.

Another determinant climatic factor is the influence of the two oceans. With the notable exception of the Yucatan peninsula, covered with a thin tropical forest which becomes firstly thorn and then savannah as we go northwards, the Atlantic zone, washed with frequent and abundant rainfall, is carpeted with dense tropical forests containing many species of huge evergreen trees and a wealth of wildlife. The much less pluvial Pacific zone, on the other hand, harbours forests of deciduous trees in greatly fewer varieties. The coastal plains are covered with forests of stocky thorn and savannah. The buffer between these two zones, a

high mountain range, often broken into several parallel lines, curves taut like a bow. This central Meso-american bow has an average altitude of 1 800 m and many outstanding ranges. It stretches upwards from the central Mexican tableland, runs southeast through southern Mexico, Guatemala and El Salvador, where the peaks above 3 000 m bristle with magnificent forests of pine and oak, dips towards Nicaragua before rising again into Costa Rica and finally disappearing into Panama. Deer, bears, opossums and wolves roam free along these heights and the high plateaux, with their lateritic red and volcanic black earth, support stands of semi-tropical forest interspersed with vast expanses of chaparral.

The Pacific coast is still very largely wild. The tropical forest often overhangs the shoreline where,
in places such as here on the Costa del Balsamo in El Salvador, fishermen set up temporary villages.

*Another aspect of the Mesoamerican coasts, the idyllic shores of the Chetumal lagoon whose waters,
shared by Mexico and Belize, mingle with the Caribbean.*

The numerous monkeys, protected by the foliage, seem to be resisting human impact on the forests better than most other species.

The world's most beautiful tropical forest

Today's tropical rain forest
is the end result of a long process which began
almost 200 million years ago when the Earth
emerged from a long period of drought to once again
enjoy the benefits of a warm, wet climate.
Luxuriant forests quickly sprouted over most of the
Pangaea (the land area including the landmasses of
the southern and northern hemispheres),
evolving down through the ages to give birth
to the stands of timber we have inherited.

The massacre

The primitive forests of Pangaea were very different from those we know today. The phanerogams (seeding or flowering plants) which include most of our present species, did not yet exist and their place was occupied by tree ferns, Cycadales and gigantic conifers whose branches formed an overhead canopy. The phanerogams, descended from the ferns, appeared a little over 100 million years ago at the time when the Pangaea was splitting into the two super-continents, Eurasia and Gondwana, which in turn broke into our present continents. The forests continued to develop, retaining only such few survivors of their primeval ranks such as the tree fern and the araucaria. To try and estimate what remains of the primitive tropical rain forest is pure guesswork. Climatic changes, natural degradation and human destruction of the environment have considerably modified the landscape. Tropical rain forest (original or naturally 'reconstructed') today

covers part of the south-eastern half of Central America, from the Mexican Chiapas to the Panamanian Darien, where it blends into the South American forest, running through Peten, the southern Yucatan, Belize, Honduras, the northern two-thirds of Nicaragua and Costa Rica. It represents one of the largest forested areas on the globe, second only to the Amazon basin, and is characterized by its exceptional biocœnosis or ecological community of species. The concentration of wildlife and plant life, influenced by Central America's very special shape as a narrow link between the northern and southern ecosystems, is one of the richest in the world.

When the Europeans arrived, the forest covered almost 90% of the Mesoamerican territory. Random clearance to gain ever more farming land and pastures for flocks, combined with the growing demand for building materials and raw materials for industry, have, in the course of less than four centuries, led to the loss of around 40% of that forest, notably over the last few decades.

Between 1950 and 1999, the situation has become catastrophic, with the destruction of a further 20% in certain countries. El Salvador is the worst case, with now only 5% of its original forest, the highest pollution level on the whole American continent and some of the weakest environmental protection laws. Despite official speeches, ecological considerations come a poor third behind special interest lobbies and industrial programmes.

A tiny settlement in Belize's Mango Creek region.
Like most inhabitants of these high hills, the villagers are forced to destroy the surrounding forest to survive.

Slash-and-burn agriculture has destroyed great tracts of forest to create cultivated fields.
Once abandoned, these are taken over by the thin, scrubby vegetation seen here in the Talamanca Cordillera in Panama.

Our modern world applies increasing pressure on the tropical rain forests. The foremost (and most widespread) danger to them are the breadline populations with high birthrates who not only need wood to build their houses, manufacture their tools or burn as fuel, but who also ravage the forests with anarchic clearance. Slash-and-burn farming destroys the ecosystem definitively. The peasants rapidly abandon the land which is soon exhausted in these tropical latitudes, moving elsewhere to begin the process over again. The second cause of massive forest destruction is the economic requirement of the conglomerates who use wood to manufacture paper, for example, or prefabricated industrial units. Great roads are opened through the forest to give access to oil drilling or mining sites or to the huge plantations of rubber, coffee, cardamom or cocoa bean. The most heart-rending feature of these operations is the sheer wastage. Thousands of uprooted trees are abandoned every day by the roadside and left to rot and many are even burned on the

spot. In Honduras alone, it is estimated that every year almost 340 million dollars' worth of timber goes up in smoke. Mexico has destroyed half of its rain forests in the course of the last thirty years. With the exception of Belize, still relatively scarcely populated and thus not yet subject to industrial pressures, most of the Mesoamerican countries lose between 500 and 1 000 square kilometres of their wooded surface every year. In percentage terms, the annual loss in Central America is much greater than in the Amazon, the subject of much more media focus.

The world seems quite indifferent to this massive and criminal deforestation, to this depletion of our common heritage. And criminal it is, because it means the programmed death of the world's richest ecosystem. Indeed, the Mesoamerican forest shelters almost half of the plant and animal species of our planet, species which are paradoxically extremely numerous overall, but which are composed of only a few representatives of each. This great variety thus comes at the cost of a great fragility. Since each species occupies a specific ecological niche which constitutes an indispensable link in the biological chain, anything which threatens one and causes it to disappear also threatens all the others.

The countries of Central America have begun to take action against the systematic destruction of their

The forests of Central America shelter practically half the known plant species in the whole world and each day brings fresh discoveries…

primitive forests by setting up, with great fanfares of publicity, a system of national parks, botanical sanctuaries and nature reserves. Honduras now has 40 protected zones (including 20 national parks), El Salvador has 4 (two of which are national parks), Costa Rica has some 60 reserves (including 21 national parks) and Panama a total of 16 national parks. The number of these protected zones is less significant, however, than the overall area they cover. Examined in this light, Costa Rica now protects almost 27% of its territory, Panama 22% and El Salvador less than 2%! The battle is obviously still far from won.

The tropical climate allows the forest to limit the damage provoked by human activity.
A dam wall of trees, always ready to spill over, surrounds all the fields and plantations.

*In the velvet green setting of the lush western Honduran forests,
the magnificent Pulhapanzak falls break the course of the Rio Lindo.*

El Salvador's Lake Coatepeque fills an ancient crater, six kilometres wide, on the eastern flank of the Santa Ana volcano.
Its fertile shores are surrounded by corn fields.

Two aspects of the light tropical forest on the Mexican Yucatán:
the stunted trees set against a stormy sky and one of the many cenotes or sinkholes running down through the vast northern limestone platform.

The Yucatan forest
and coastal mangroves of Central America

Comprising the Mexican states of Yucatan, Quintana Roo and the northern part of Campeche, the Yucatan peninsula is a huge limestone platform, dating from the late Tertiary, some 150 metres on average above sea level. Its dry, karstic surface is dotted with many cenotes, those characteristic deep sinkholes with pools of ground water at their bottom, and is covered with two distinct zones of vegetation. The southern third is carpeted with wet tropical forest whereas the much drier northern two-thirds, watered with less than 150 mm of rainfall a year, is covered with a light tropical forest. The little rain the northern part receives falls mainly between June and September, leaving the vegetation to survive on drought rations for the rest of the year. This dearth of water is further aggravated by the fact that the peninsula stretches into the sea like a rock, with no streams or rivers worth mentioning. Thus we find a low, dry vegetation made up of thorn and semi-deciduous or deciduous trees. These latter species are the most

The huge evergreens of the wet forests bordering Belize's New River herald
the vast rain forests of Central America.

common and the light forest of the Yucatan fades to yellow during the drought months to turn green again when the rains return. Depending on local climatic and geological particularities, it may be denser, like open parkland, or sparser, in the form of veldt with scattered trees. Birds, monkeys and butterflies populate what little forest canopy there is while the scrubby undergrowth below is inhabited by a host of little mammals (rodents, coatis, anteaters...) and insects. Around the coasts of the peninsula, notably along its

northern edge, the vegetation thins to a dry savannah punctuated with thorn trees and xeric shrubs. The southern half of the Quintana Roo coastline, on the other hand, is scattered with mangroves, harbingers of the great swamps down in Belize.

The mangrove is ubiquitous in Central America. Although not so common in Mexico, where it is mainly found on the southern tip of Baja California and along the Pacific coast between Puerto Vallarta and the Gulf of Tehuantepec, it covers almost all of the Caribbean shoreline, spreads along the Gulf of Honduras, up the Belize coast, over all the encouragingly-named 'Mosquito' region (*la Mosquitia* in Honduras, Nicaragua's *Mosquito Coast*, the Costa Rican *Gulf of Mosquitoes* and Panama) and extends over many parts of the Pacific coast, notably from Ocos to Champeco and from Sipacate to Iztapa in Guatemala, over most of the El Salvadoran and all of the Honduran shoreline, the northern half of the Nicaraguan coast, the Gulf of Nicoya in Costa Rica, the region south of David (included in the Gulf of Chiriqui national park),

The Mesoamerican tropical forests are home to the world's richest diversity of wildlife. Prized for its tawny-grey spotted fur, the ocelot is threatened by over-intensive hunting whereas the tapir, sometimes attaining 440 pounds, weighs in as the subcontinent's largest land mammal.

many sections of the Azuero peninsula and, of course, all the Darien coast in Panama. The mangrove coasts are a special type of tropical rain forest, densely wooded but with very few tree and plant species. These are mainly composed of the Rhizophoraceae family, the Avicennia, the Laguncularia and the Conocarpus, all tropical maritime trees and shrubs with the characteristic prop roots. There are also other trees, some very large (up to 30 metres in height), and shrubs which thrive on the silt-laden soils lapped by *cont. page 49*

▷

The planet's richest ecosystem, the Mesoamerican rain forest is also one of the most fragile, constantly menaced by human and natural aggressions.

Two other rain forest dwellers: the arboreal sloth, so-called because of its slow movements through the branches, and the coati, locally known as pisote, *a small carnivore with a flexible snout and a taste for larvae and insects.*

The warm, wet climate fosters a proliferation of butterflies and insects of all sorts.
A magnificent jabiru stork spreads his wings to show his irritation.

▷

*Practically impenetrable to man,
the secret and fascinating world
of the mangroves.
Colonies of birds and large reptiles,
like this crocodile and iguana,
live undisturbed in these havens.*

*The treetops remain the stronghold for birds, as these weavers whose nests are seen above, monkeys, such as this spider monkey with her baby,
and other mammals like this raccoon, one of the species most hunted for their fur.*

A male howler monkey proclaims his territorial supremacy with long piercing cries.
Sacred for the ancient Mayas, this animal is now threatened by forest destruction.

the salt waters of the shoreline. The various species have adapted to this special environment, notably those in direct contact with the sea, developing pneumatophores or roots which function as respiratory organs when the ground is flooded. The mangrove swamps shelter their own special wildlife which includes crabs, shellfish, snakes and turtles in the wetter parts and an extraordinarily rich diversity, on all levels, on the land side: aquatic insects on the forest floor, reptiles and amphibians in the branches and colonies of nesting birds in the treetops.

Belize's Caribbean coastline features some of the finest stands of mangrove,
as here in the Shipstem region.

*The dark and uninviting mass of the great cloud forest, dotted with tree ferns,
seen here in the Braulio Carrillo national park in Costa Rica.*

The rain and cloud forests

Stretching over 2 200 kilometres from North to South, a long series of forests cover the Chiapas and the southern third of the Mexican Yucatan, western Belize, the Guatemalan Peten, the central regions of Honduras and Nicaragua, Costa Rica and Panama. As their name suggests, these tropical rain forests grow in a constantly wet environment. Rainfall is distributed regularly throughout the year and the annual measure never falls below 2 000 mm (an astonishing two metres of water a year!). Tropical forests include the actual rain forests themselves, which remain the same all year round, and what are called the peripheral tropical forests, which change with the seasons. They may be divided geographically into two categories: the rain forests on the plains, averaging 900 m above sea level but sometimes climbing to 1 200 m, and the tropical forest at altitude, poetically known as 'cloud forests', growing between 900 m and 2 000 m, where they give way to the conifers (this upper limit sometimes exceptionally extended to 2 500 m).

The plain forests are by far the most extensive but, because more easily accessible, the most heavily logged. They are evergreen, the various species of trees keeping their leaves all year round or at least shedding them at different times. The heavy foliage filters most of the sunlight and allows the undergrowth and soil to remain moist. Humidity often attains 80%, temperatures never fall below 20°C and the sunlight penetration rarely exceeds 2% at ground level. These special factors give a double or triple-tiered vegetation with, in some cases, other, intermediary layers. At ground level and up to a height of 2 to 3 metres, we find a dense carpet of ground-hugging plants, annuals, shrubs and scrub, all of which grow in abundance despite the general poverty of tropical soils. The middle level is made up of medium-sized trees (trumpet-trees, palms, figs, mahogany and chicle-yielding sapodillas) which try to fight their way to the light through the lianas and lower branches of the forest giants. To understand their difficulties, we should remember that in a tropical forest, 8% of the vegetable species are climbing plants and another 15 500 species, an enormous 25%, are epiphytic, deriving their moisture from the atmosphere rather than the ground and generally growing on other plants. The top floor of the forest is the canopy, made up of tightly interlocking branches generally between 35 to 45 metres above the ground. This canopy is pierced by the real giants, some towering to 60 metres, technically known as emergents. These include many species with rigid leaves and buttressed bases (such as kapok trees) whose tops look down on the sea of green around them and whose trunks shoot up straight, like the piers of cathedrals, for around 40 metres before the first branches radiate off into the canopy. The animal life of the forest is also broken down into several levels. On the ground floor live the large mammals (jaguars, ocelots, tayras, peccaries, tapirs...), the major reptiles (alligators, crocodiles, iguanas...), the rodents, the anteaters, the armadillos and the insects (ants, termites...). In the middle we find the snakes and the small reptiles, the tree frogs and certain marsupials. The canopy is the realm of the butterflies, the monkeys and sloths whereas the emergents are reserved for the birds, the bats and the flying insects. Some very beautiful rain forests do still exist, including primary forest in certain protected zones. The most representative are to be found in the national parks of Pico Bonito and Punta Sal in Honduras, those of Corcovado, Braulio Carrillo and La Amistad in Costa Rica and, especially, the Darien Park in Panama which, with its 5 800 square kilometres, is the largest in Central America.

The cloud forest, colder than the rain forest all year round, is wetter still, with a humidity rating of almost 99%! It owes its name to the fact that the rain falls practically daily and that a heavy mist rarely lifts from the upper branches. Because temperatures fall as the land rises (between 0.5 and 0.7° for each 100 m in altitude), the canopy lowers as we climb higher. It rarely exceeds 30 metres for a lower mountain forest (900 to 1 600 m) and drops to 15 metres for the highlands above. The characteristic root buttresses and the cauliflorous vegetation (with flowers growing straight from the main stem) of the tropical rain forest disappear and we find ourselves in a world of moss, lichen, orchids, Spanish moss and ferns which become increasingly tree-like as we move upwards. The forest floor, soaked like a sponge and kept in a permanent twilight, is covered with a carpet of vegetable debris (leaves, fallen trunks, sections of lianas) which rots much more slowly than in a rain forest. This slow rotting process generates a layer of acid compost which emprisons the available nutrients and so impoverishes the soil. The trees are often stunted and twisted but the wildlife is still abundant. A wide variety of small mammals, of seed and fruit-eating birds (including the legendary quetzal) and of insects live in this twilight world. The finest stands of cloud forest in Central America are found in Honduras (national parks of Celaque, Cerro Azul, Cusuco, Montana de Comayagua, *cont. page 55*

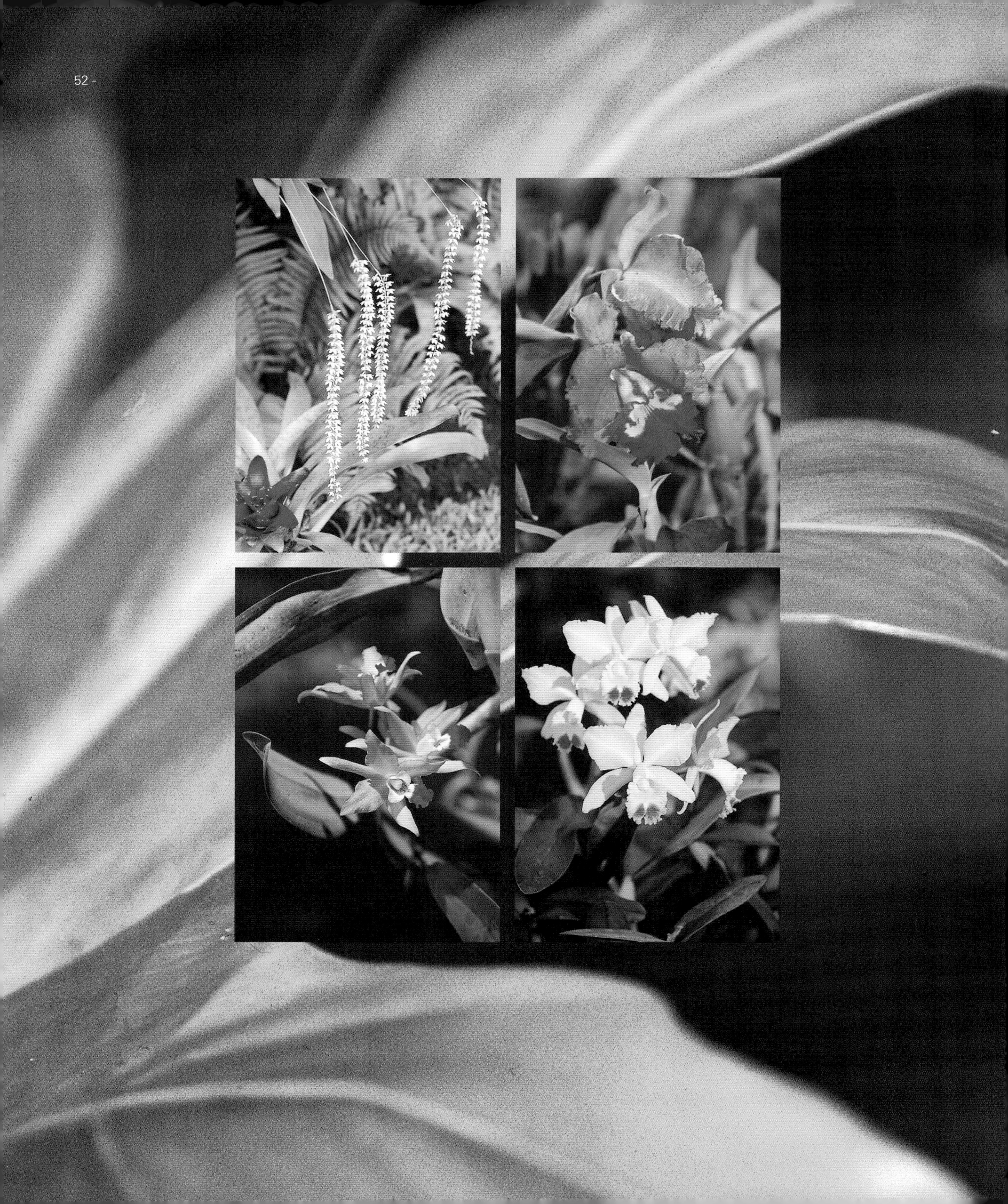

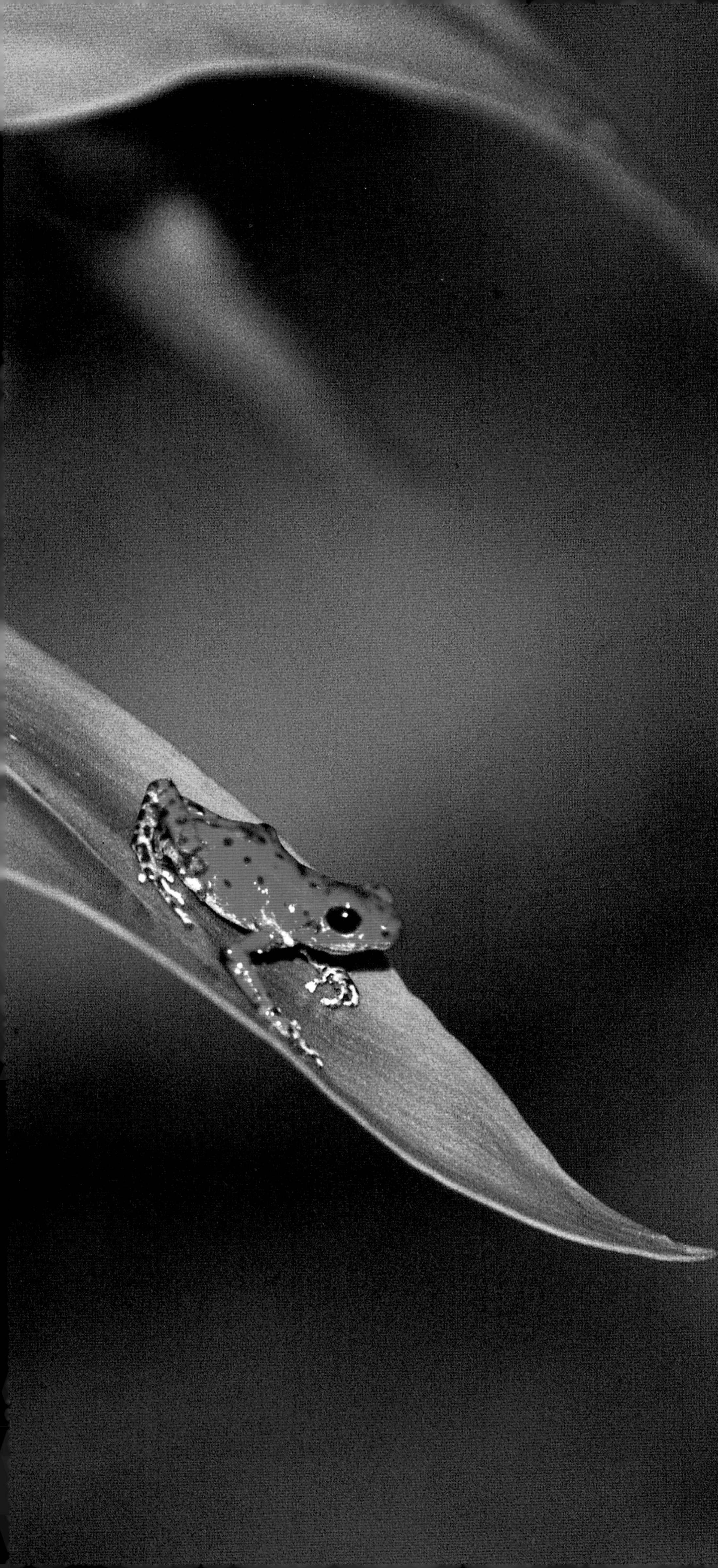

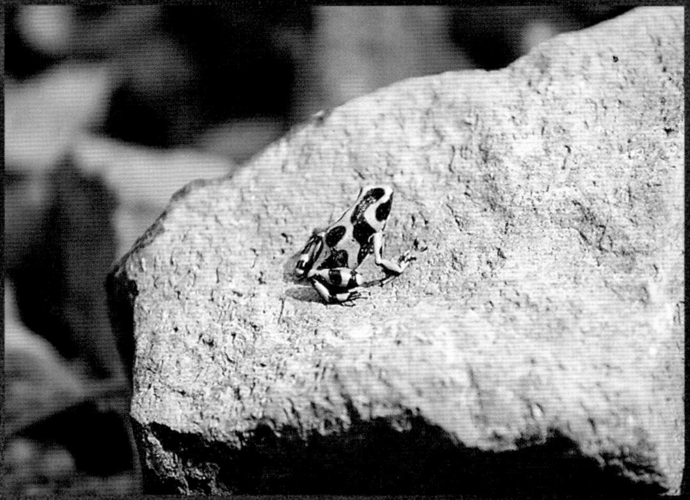

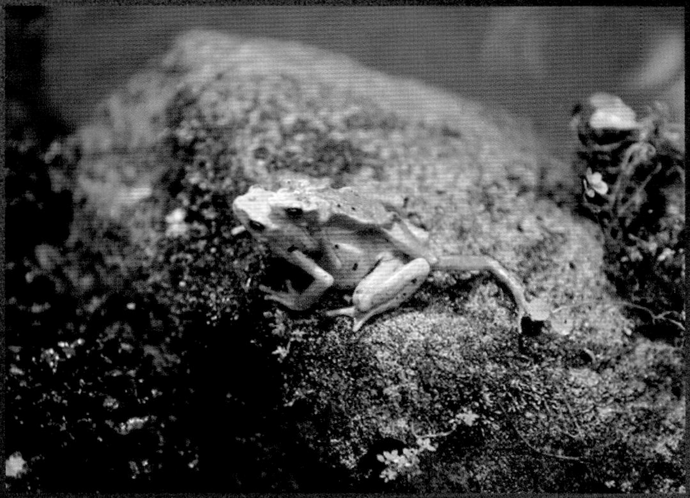

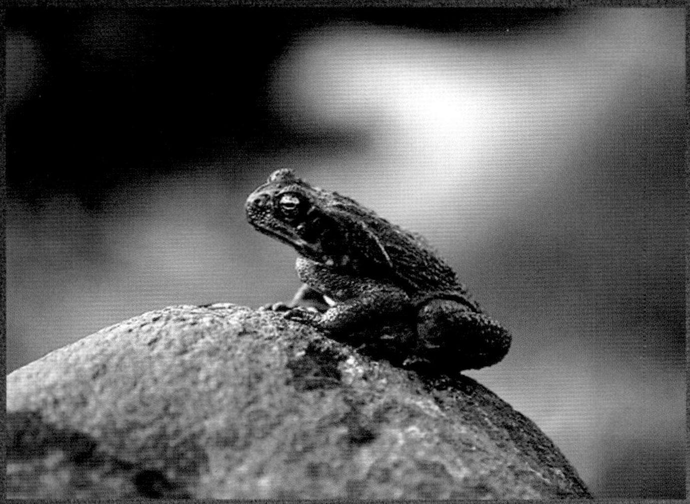

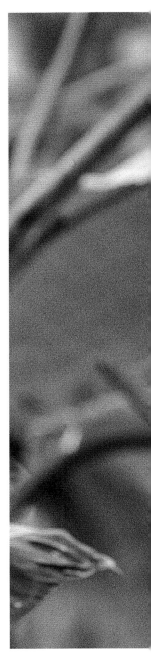

The biodiversity of the tropical rain and cloud forests of Central America is beyond comparison.
They contain, among other treasures, the world's greatest concentrations of orchids and amphibians.

This member of the deer family and the great hocco, a flightless bird,
belong to two species very much threatened today by hunting and destruction of their forest habitat.

Montana de Toro, Montecristo-Trifinio, Pico Pijol, Santa Barbara...) and in northern Nicaragua (all the regions watered by the Coco, the Bocay and the Waskup rivers) - all of which are regions sparsely populated by Central American standards. There are also magnificent cloud forests in Costa Rica, all in the protected zones of Monteverde, Volcan Poas and Chirripo.

A few figures suffice to give some idea of the wealth of flora and fauna of a tropical rain or cloud forest in

Central America. Specialists have counted around one million *known* vegetable and animal species but agree that other millions will be discovered as we study the forest. In Costa Rica alone, they have recorded 10,000 different vascular plants, 1 250 species of orchids, 1 500 different trees, 220 species of mammals, 880 species of birds (including over 50 types of hummingbirds), a stunning 36,000 species of insects, 170 species of amphibians, 225 species of reptiles... and the same is true for all the surrounding countries. To say that Central America possesses the world's most beautiful tropical forest is almost an understatement.

With a wingbeat so fast the human eye can barely see it, this tiny hummingbird hovers in flight,
probing flowers with its long bill to feed on the nectar.

This parchment, preserved in the Cortes Palace in Cuernavaca (Mexico), shows the arrival of the Spanish conquistadores in Central America.

The discovery of the New World

Until the 15th century,
official learning and religious dogma
denied any possibility that there might be
lands west of the Atlantic Ocean.
Yet since antiquity, legends and accounts
had whispered the contrary.
In 1492, a certain Christopher Columbus
brought back the triumphant confirmation
that the American continent
was a solid reality.

The pre-Columbian voyages

In the new light of various discoveries, it is now agreed that Europeans and perhaps even before them, voyagers from the Middle East or Japan, landed in various regions of the American continent well before Columbus. Thus the Carthaginian Hamilcon, in the 5th century BC, claims to have sailed on a "great western sea covered with floating weeds" which may well have been the Sargasso Sea. Many tales dip into legend and it is very difficult to winnow the truth from pure storytelling. To see our way a little more clearly through the mists and myths of the western ocean, we have to wait until the 5th century AD for the accounts from Irish literature. The Celtic epics of the seafarers from these times onwards provide us with a great deal of interesting information. The most famous narrate the adventures of explorers who set out westwards across the ocean: Bran, whose voyage lasted "several centuries", Maelduin, who sailed for three years and seven months, and St. Brendan, who wished to carry the Christian doctrine to the peoples "situated across the Great Sea". What is interesting in these stories is not so much whether their heroes actually existed but rather their confirmation that Welsh and Irish sailors used to go and seek, ever farther westwards, between the 6th and the 11th centuries, the lands they called by magical names like Mag Mell ("Plain of Happiness") or Tyr nan Og ("Land of Eternal Youth").

With today's knowledge, we can neither confirm nor deny that the Celts managed to land on the American continent, but we can be certain that the Vikings achieved the exploit around the year 1000. The Icelandic sagas tell how one of their groups, led by Erik the Red, banished from Iceland after some serious conflicts there, came to settle in Greenland. Leif Erikson, their leader's son, left the new settlement at the head of an expedition which seems to have arrived in North America around the late 10th century and which, according to their accounts, discovered Hellulandia ("Country of Stone"), Marklandia ("Country of Wood") and Vinlandia ("Land of Vines"), names which must have corresponded with zones located in the centre and North of the present-day United States. Other narratives speak of expeditions led by figures less well known - Bjarin, Thorfin or Karlsefin - in the early 11th century. Archæologists and historians have discovered traces of these Scandinavian settlements in the north of today's United States and in the Canadian Arctic. Taking, as its starting point, the existence of cairn beacons on the great islands of northern Canada (Baffin, Bathurst, Cornwallis…) and the presence of Nordic European elements in certain north-Amerindian cultures, one theory has it that some groups of Vikings, driven out of Greenland by the wars of religion, founded colonies along the American coasts, thereby giving birth to the famous tribes of "white Indians" (the Mandans of Missouri and Ohio, the Tuscaroras of Virginia, the Tunits of Labrador, the Mizamichis of Quebec's Gaspé Peninsula and others) which the 16th century pilgrims sought so eagerly to discover.

In the meantime, the West had lifted its head and widened its psychological horizon. In the 13th century, Marco Polo's Book of Marvels was a literary sensation and in the 15th century, Pope Pius II, a keen astronomer and mathematician, supported the thesis that the world was round at a time when the Portuguese were putting the final touches to their portolanos, the finest marine charts ever produced. The sea road to official discovery of the American continent was now wide open to any courageous enough to attempt it. One man was and did: Christopher Columbus.

The adventure of Christopher Columbus

Everything began in the port of Palos. On Friday, the 2nd of August 1492, three little ships, the Santa Maria, the Pinta and the Nina, set out with a crew of ninety seamen and some thirty servants and administrative staff under the orders of Admiral Columbus to conquer new lands in the name of their Very Catholic Majesties, Ferdinard II of Aragon and Isabella I of Castile. After long weeks of difficult navigation, the expedition first reached the Bahamas archipelago before finally landing on Cuba and Haiti. The Admiral believed he had reached India and thus called the inhabitants Indians. After a short stay, he decided to return to Europe to give an account of his mission.

And so, in 1493, we find him again before Ferdinand and Isabella, this time for an interview which gave rise to one of the dark passages in history. Admiral Columbus lied when he affirmed to the royal couple and the assembled court that there was a wealth of gold in the new territories, that there were precious stones

The ruins of the fort of Portobelo, in Panama, stand near the spot where Christopher Columbus landed in 1502.
They were part of the imposing line of fortresses the Spanish erected between the 16th and 17th centuries
to defend themselves against maurading pirates, notably the British.

and mines galore and that the locals asked nothing more than to become the good and loyal servants of their Very Catholic Majesties. The Genoese certainly distorted the truth in the aim of returning to the New World. His desire to return was so overpowering that, it would seem, he never realized that his words, once the Spanish sovereigns had finished expressing their gratitude towards him, were to trigger one of the most bloody episodes in our history, the Conquest...

Christopher Columbus set off again from Cadiz on his second voyage on the 25th of September 1493, this time with 17 ships and 1500 men. He reconnoitred several of the Caribbean islands, inhabited by cannibalistic peoples (Dominica, Guadeloupe and Jamaica), before continuing his exploration of Cuba. His management of these new territories was vigorously contested by the nobility who considered him a common foreigner and, by order, he was brought back to Spain in chains. Once again his charm had its effect on the sovereigns, who freed him and then received him in Granada where they heard him plead his case. They decided to take charge of the territories annexed by Columbus and abrogated several clauses of the *capitulacion* of 1492. Despite opposition from the nobility, they allowed their admiral to depart a third time for the New World in 1498 on an expedition which was to last two years. Columbus desperately wished to reach the continent to the west of the Caribbean islands but the king of Spain had forbidden him to do so. Destiny had decided that the Genoese was not to be the first European to set foot on American soil. Between 1499 and 1500, several expeditions, led by former shipmates, followed the trail he had blazed

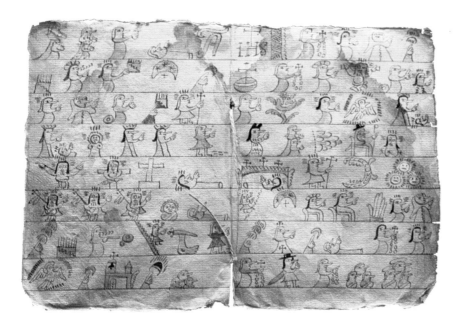 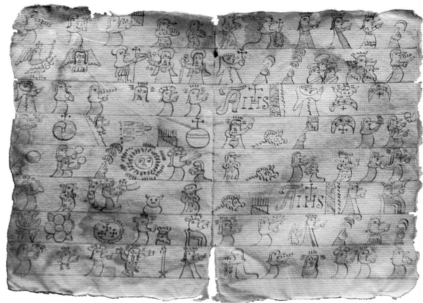

and reached the mythical continent where they explored some 5 000 kilometres of coastline down to the Isthmus of Panama. One of them, Alonso de Ojeda, had on board two seamen of outstanding worth, Juan de la Cosa and the Florentine-born Amerigo Vespucci who went ashore on the northern coast of South America (Guyana and Venezuela). Many years later, the great continent thus discovered was named after the intrepid Florentine. Back in Spain, a disappointed man, ill-considered in court yet undefeated, Columbus managed to have himself appointed in charge of a fourth and final royal squadron. He left in 1502 with 4 ships and 140 men, this time for the continent. By order of the king, he was to seek a strait to help trade and a site where a Spanish colony might settle. He was thus the first to enter into contact, albeit briefly, with the Mexican peoples, the Mayas of the Yucatan, and the Indian populations in Honduras, Nicaragua, Costa Rica and Panama. After having claimed Costa Rica and Panama in the name of the Spanish crown, he returned across the ocean in 1504. Queen Isabella died shortly after his return, leaving him bereft of his ever-faithful protectress. Despite his protests and his pleas to recover his former privileges or at least be left with those remaining to him, he was forgotten by the king and died in undeserved semi-disgrace.
The following centuries were to restore his honour, however, and in the eyes of the world he remains the man who discovered America.

Illustrations from the 16th and 17th centuries
offer precious glimpses of the early colonial period.

*This fresco in the Vargas park in Puerto Limon (Costa Rica) gives some idea of the image the present inhabitants
of Central America retain of their pre-Columbian past.*

The colonisation of Central America

The American continent had barely been discovered when expeditions were organised from bases established by the Spanish in the Caribbean, notably in Haiti and Cuba. The hostility of the natives was such, however, that none of these attempts succeeded in establishing any permanant settlement on the mainland. When Nicolas de Ovando was authorized to mount a large-scale expedition in 1502, the Spanish crown clearly indicated its wish to colonize and occupy the new territories. Vincente Yanez Pinzon disembarked on the northern coast of Honduras in 1508. The following year, the first Spanish trading post in Latin America was founded west of the Gulf of Uraba, at the present border between Panama and Colombia, before being rapidly transferred to Santa Maria de la Antigua del Darien, generally known as Darien. That same year, the crown again began granting licences to Spanish captains, thereby triggering the wholesale conquest of Central America from northern Mexico down to southern Panama. Diego de Nicuesa, a Spaniard who had already made a fortune from the mines in Haiti, was given the mission of reconnoitring the region lying between the isthmus and Cape Gracias a Dios, a huge stretch of land corresponding to today's Nicaragua, Costa Rica and Panama. Beset with tropical illnesses and constantly assailed by the natives, his expedition

was a disaster. Sent in charge of a search party, another captain finally found him with forty haggard survivors and brought them all back to Darien. The mayor of this outpost, one Vasco Nunez de Balboa, was himself an intrepid captain who had explored many archipelagos and who, with his wise and humane administrative approach, had forged special bonds of trust with the native peoples. In 1513, he trekked across the isthmus and discovered the "Great Southern Sea" (the future Pacific), a revelation which was to open the route to South America for other conquistadores. In his absence, others plotted against him and he was replaced as governor in 1513 by Pedro Arias de Avila, who had him beheaded three years later. Darien's new strongman, known as Pedrarias, consolidated his grip on the region, often with considerable brutality, and founded Panama, the city which was to serve as the home base for the conquest of South America.

In the North, the saga of discovery began with the trading expeditions of Francisco Hernandez de Cordoba in 1517 and those of Juan de Grijalva the following year. Arriving on the Mexican shore, the Europeans were attacked by Indians and had to beat a hasty retreat. In 1519, the sea captain Hernan Cortes left Cuba with 11 ships carrying 550 men and 16 horses. He first disembarked in Yucatan before setting off again towards the Gulf of Campeche where his first contacts with the local people, the Totonaques, were encouraging. He soon realized, however, that the entire region lived in fear of the all-powerful Anahuac empire, the Aztecs. Meetings and exchanges of presents were arranged with the Aztec ruler, Montezuma II Xocoyotzin, but conflict was inevitable. Tenochtitlan, the Aztec capital, fell into the hands of the Spanish on the night of August 13th 1521 after a day of terrible combat and Cuauhtemoc, the young man who had become emperor the year before when his brother died, was taken prisoner. Once rebuilt, the city became the capital of New Spain, as Mexico was then known. The Spanish, convinced of the existence of a hidden Aztec treasure,

The violence and ferocity of the Spanish conquest stand out in these two paintings
by Diego de Rivera in Mexico City's Cortes Palace.

subjected Cuauhtemoc and the nobles to dreadful tortures before finally executing them four years later.

Cortes then proceeded with the second phase of his conquest. He sent two of his principal lieutenants, the bloodthirsty Pedro de Alvarado in 1524 and Cristobal de Olid in 1525, to secure the Spanish hold on the lands to the south of New Spain. The former, assisted by a strong detachment of Aztec warriors, began his (in)famous crusade into Guatemala, then a part of New Spain. With the decisive battle of Quetzaltenango in 1524, the door into central Guatemala and, thence, into El Salvador and Honduras was wrenched open and de Alvarado went on to conquer all these lands with his customary savagery... for the greater glory of his Spanish sovereigns and the Christian faith. Aside from the taking of Tenochtitlan, no other episode in the conquest had such a marked effect on the native mind as the subjugation of Guatemala. Cortes's other lieutenant, Cristobal de Olid, reached Honduras and established the town of Trujillo on the site where Columbus had reached land in 1502. He went on to take the islands to the north and the country inland when, seized by some sudden ambition, he decided to break with Cortes. The latter left Mexico immediately to march south and deal with the insurrection. Having accomplished his purpose, he returned to Mexico leaving Spanish leaders behind him who immediately began to fight one another for domination over this country where gold had just been found. Pedro de Alvarado went to settle the matter in his usual style, eliminating almost all contenders. In 1524, Comayagua supplanted Trujillo as capital and Honduras was put under the tutelage of the Captaincy General of Guatemala.

During this time, expeditions were setting out regularly from Panama. Pedrarias had first sent ships to reconnoitre the Atlantic and Pacific shorelines up towards the Northwest. In 1522, the conquistador Gil Gonzales de Avila landed in Nicaragua, where he made friendly contact with the Nicaraos, while one of his lieutenants, Andres Nino, continued up to the Gulf of Fonseca. Two years later, another expedition, commanded by Francisco Hernandez de Cordoba, founded the city of Granada and then that of Leon. From these two new bases, the Spanish launched several expeditions which enabled them to take control of the country which then became another part of the Captaincy General of Guatemala.

Arriving from Nicaragua in 1522, Gil Gonzales de Avila was again the first to establish bridgeheads on the territory of today's El Salvador but the real conqueror of the country was Cortes's lieutenant, Pedro de Alvarado, who had continued his march southwards after having subdued Guatemala. He founded the town of San Salvador de Cuscatlan, forever afterwards abridged to San Salvador and destined to become the capital. Shortly before this, in the western part of Nicaragua, the Spanish soldiers had met up with the force led by Cortes to punish Cristobal de Olid and his rebels. Spain now ruled over an immense territory stretching from Mexico to Darien. Panama served as a beachhead for the conquest of South America and was thus included into New Granada (the name then given to Colombia) in the early 17th century.

Things went differently in Costa Rica, the last country to be colonised, and Belize, which was almost never colonised by the Spanish. In the course of his fourth voyage, Christopher Columbus was the first European to set foot on Costa Rican soil. This was in 1502, near the present-day Puerto Limon. He stayed there for only seventeen days, but was so impressed by the gold ornaments and jewellery of the natives that he baptised the region 'Rich Coast' or Costa Rica. Diego de Nicuesa became governor of the country four years later but all attempts at colonisation failed miserably in the face of determined native hostility. It was not until 1560 that Costa Rica, under the hegemony of the Audiencia of Guatemala, began another phase of colonisation. In 1561, Juan de Cavallon managed to set up a few Spanish trading posts and Vasquez de Coronado followed suit two years later. Yet despite their efforts, the land remained for almost two centuries the New World's poor relation in the eyes of a crown which showed little interest in this little backwater covered with impenetrable forests and peopled with hostile savages. Belize, on the other hand, was a very different matter. This sparsely populated zone of the Mayan Marches, although officially belonging to New Spain, offered no particular riches and was thus almost continually neglected by the Spanish. English and Scottish pirates seized the opportunity of established strongholds there from the very beginning of the 1660s and in 1798, following the defeat of the Spanish fleet by British gunboats, Belize saw the Union Jack hoisted in anticipation of an official transfer of sovereignty some sixty years later. Shortly afterwards, taking advantage of the Civil War and the United States's consequent temporary inability to enforce the Monroe Doctrine (the 1853 statement of US foreign policy opposing all European interference in the western hemisphere), London transformed Belize, or British Honduras as it was now known, into a colony, encouraging citizens from all over the Empire to come and settle there.

2
The legacy of former gods

The Mesoamerican region has nurtured the highest concentration of cultures and produced the most brilliant civilizations on the American continent. A culture is what we might term all the socio-political structures, the artistic creations and religious observations which distinguish one ethnic group from another. A civilization, on the other hand, is the final flowering of a culture brought to the highest degree and, as such, needs no comparison with others.

◁ *This polychrome statue is part of a collection of objects recently discovered on the Mayan site of Lamanaï in Belize.*

The pre-Classic radiance of the Olmec civilization

Born of the slow maturation
of various prehistoric cultures, the Mesoamerican
pre-Classic encompasses a very long period
stretching from 2500 BC to around 250 AD.
Beginning somewhere about 1200 BC,
the Olmecs, a people whose origins are still unclear,
established the first American civilization on
the shores of the Gulf of Mexico.
Its influence was to have a profound effect on all
the civilizations which were to succeed it.

One of the monumental heads with mysteriously negroid features dating from the Olmec civilization.

The finest cave paintings in Central America are to be found in Baja California (Mexico),
as these here from the Cueva de Los Palmitos near San Ignacio.

From the Neolithic revolution to the first crops

The American continent was the last on which Man settled. His presence there is not attested until some 22,000 years ago in Canada, 21,000 in Mexico, 18,000 in Peru and 11,000 in Tierra del Fuego, a series of datings which indicates that the first bands of Asian hunters trekked from Siberia over to Alaska, taking advantage of the drop in ocean levels caused by the glaciation to cross the Bering Strait, and gradually drifted southwards in search of game. There were several of these waves of Asian migrations, the last necessarily being prior to the eighth millenary BC when rising global temperatures melted the ice sheets and thereby submerged the convenient land bridge. Other minority groups of immigrants (Japanese, Chinese, Filipinos, Malay-Polynesians and, perhaps, Australians…) later crossed the Pacific to complete the American ethnic panorama. This extraordinary human adventure is still cloaked in mystery and still poses many unanswered questions. The bands of primitive nomads must have had to adapt to the climatic differences between the freezing northlands and the steaming heat of the tropical forests. And then again readjust to the bitterly cold forests of southern South America. They must have changed their diets when certain great mammals, like the mammoths, disappeared between 9000 and 7000 years ago. The small populations of Paleolithic hunter-gatherers lived a predatory existence which must have led them to cross the wet meadows of the high valleys in search of food.

About 7000 BC, a considerable rise in world temperatures modified living conditions on the American continent and favoured the first agricultural experiments (in Mexico's Tehuacan Valley, for example). Mesolithic man gradually forsook his former way of life, remaining semi-nomadic but beginning to see the advantages of husbandry and, especially, starting to domesticate wild cereals. When, later, societies were created with economies really based on herding and agriculture (notably cereals, including Indian corn, but also squash or marrows, pumpkins, beans and other crops), this was the beginning of the Neolithic revolution, a new age characterized by sedentary farming. 5000 years later, crops included avocados, chillies and many varieties of fruit. It is generally thought that the famous American 'nutritive trilogy' of squash-corn-beans became standard fare in Mesoamerica in the late 3rd millenary BC, just before the appearance of weaving and, later, pottery.

All these generations of primitive humans left traces of their passing. There are many rock art sites in Mexico, Nicaragua and Costa Rica. Human figures, hunting and praying, and animals (monkeys, deer, mountain goats, snakes, lizards, turtles and fish) abound in the caves and canyons of Baja California, including such famous sites as Cueva del Raton, Cueva Pintada, Cueva de las Flechas, Cueva de los Palmitos, Cueva San Borgita and the San Juan Rock, in the state of Chihuahua near Casas Grandes (Arroyo de los Monos) and Madera (Cueva Grande), and in the state of Oaxaca (the burial shelters of Mitla and those around Oaxaca). The southern regions of Central America also boast remarkable examples of rupestrian art, notably in Nicaragua, near Managua, on the island of Omotepe and around the shores of Lake Nicaragua, and in western Panama, on the slopes of Mount Baru and in the Chiriqui region, and in the centre of the country, notably down the Azuero peninsula and in the El Valle region (the celebrated Pierra Pintada petroglyphs).

The mysterious Olmecs

Between 4000 and 2000 years BC, some cultural concentrations gained special importance, particularly in the Mexico Valley, along the Chiapas Pacific coast, in the Huaxtec and in western Honduras, on the Guatemalan Altos, in western Nicaragua and in central Panama. Around the year 1200 BC, one of these, located near the Gulf of Mexico, underwent a spectacular development which gave rise to the first Central American civilization. A people of mysterious origins created a remarkable empire and culture which dominated the lowlands of Mexico's Veracruz and Tabasco, a rich and fertile region irrigated by an abundance of streams and carpeted with luxuriant forests. We call these people the Olmecs, the "people of rubber", from the name given to them by the Aztecs. In fewer than 50 years, the local populations switched from a semi-nomadic existence to an urban way of life, transforming their hamlets into cities, their rock sanctuaries into dressed-stone temples and their animist and magical beliefs into a fully-fledged religion. The heart of the Olmec region is centred around three original sites: San Lorenzo (near Acayucan in the state of Veracruz), which flowered between 1200 and 900 BC, La Venta (in the state of Tabasco), which lived its finest years between 800 and 400 BC, and Tres Zapotes (not far from La Venta), whose development reached its zenith towards 400 BC when the Olmec empire began the decline which was to end in its abrupt disappearance a century later. The Olmec civilization radiated its influence over a vast region stretching from the Mexican Anahuac in the west to the Oaxaca valleys in the south. Some historians even speak of a real 'cultural imperialism' which largely transcended natural boundaries, citing as proof the Olmec-made giant found near Chalchuapa in western El Salvador, some 800 kilometres away. Skilled farmers and craftsmen, able builders of ceremonial centres, towns and canals, the Olmecs established a system of communications and a trading network which made them undisputed masters of the region around the Gulf of Mexico. A lighthouse in the murky pre-Classic, their civilization surpassed by far any of the achievements of other ancient cultures. The

Olmecs built a genuine empire founded on a society, divided into castes, where the arts were given a leading rôle. Among the many artistic forms we know they practised (architecture, painting, sculpture and pottery), the creations which most struck the imaginations of the following generations were their gigantic stone heads with their surprisingly negroid features. Of the dozen of these known today, some stand 3 metres high and weigh over 10 tons! Many of their inscribed stelæ have also been unearthed, together with altars and statuettes representing human figures and animals (manatees, monkeys, jaguars and others). The human effigies are characterized by their flattened noses, powerful square jaws, their thick lips often drawn back into a feline muzzle (which accounts for the name *tenocelome*, 'he with the jaguar maw', often given them) and their shortened bodies with bulging stomachs. In certain cases, the figures feature curious æsthetic anomalies such as gross obesity, dwarfism or acromegaly (hyperpituitarism giving progressive enlargement of feet, hands and face). We know that the Olmec civilization was a reign of fear, but of what? Fear of the elements? Fear of the kings and priests or of the gods? Fear of the imminent end of the world? These questions are only some of many still unanswered about the most mysterious civilization in Central America. We do not even know the real name of this people, nor what language they spoke. Nor do we know why this brilliant culture came to such a sudden end, voluntarily it would seem, in the early years of the 5th century BC.

The El Valle de Anton region in Panama abounds in prehistoric sites.
This one, nicknamed La Pintada, *contains unusual petroglyphs representing humans, animals and other motifs difficult to decipher.*

Stonecarving of a lizard from the so-called Guayabo culture in Costa Rica.
The most impressive site from this culture is the Hillocks, the remaining foundations of an ancient ceremonial complex.
On the island of Omotepe, in Nicaragua, many of the rocks dotting the flanks of the Madera volcano are engraved with spirals and solar symbols.

One of the monumental heads of the plumed serpents which decorate the lower levels of the Quetzalcoatl Temple in Teotihuacan (Mexico).

The theocratic states of the Classic period

The Classic period covers the years
from about AD 200 to 1000.
While three great civilizations, the Teotihuacan,
the Monte Alban and the El Tajinin, blossomed in
central Mexico and along the Gulf, a fourth,
destined to become the most brilliant on the entire
continent, was developing in the warm homeland
of the Mayas down in the Southeast.
This was an great era of peace, as may be seen
from the cities built without fortifications.

The majestic splendour of Teotihuacan

Central America spawned many centres of culture between the 4th and the 2nd centuries BC. In Nicaragua, the ancestors of the Chorotegas built ceremonial sites decorated with petroglyphs while, further south in Costa Rica, an unknown people founded a remarkable urban complex, served by a complete network of raised highways, on a site which had been occupied for the previous 600 years and which was to remain so for the following 1 700. Other important cultures came to light on the Caribbean coast of Belize, on the Yucatan peninsula, at the foot of the western volcanic ranges in Panama and elsewhere, yet none of them could be correctly described as a civilization.

The great civilizations of the Mesoamerican Classic period were all marked by the development of city planning, the establishment of powerful theocracies and the rapid growth of a trade system based on a network of fixed trading posts. In the middle of the 3rd century BC, in a little valley lying some forty kilometres northeast of present-day Mexico City, a people probably originally from the Gulf of Mexico began to lay the foundations of a remarkable culture, certainly the most important since the disappearance of the Olmecs. Less than a century later, it already had a highly elaborate socio-economic system and a capital city. By the end of another century or two, the latter had swollen into an immense city-state, rigorously planned, which we know only by its Aztec name of Teotihuacan, meaning 'the place where the gods live' or 'the place where the gods were created'. Now the head of a veritable trading empire, it continued to grow in size and power until the 6th century AD, wielding a cultural and economic influence which extended from Huaxtec to Guatemala. In its heyday, the capital covered 25 square kilometres and counted 200,000 inhabitants, a huge number for the period. The most colossal monuments, such as the Pyramid of the Sun (the third largest in the world after those of Cholula in Mexico and Khufu in Egypt), the Pyramid of the Moon and the Temple of Quetzalcoatl, were built between the 1st and the 4th centuries AD using new architectural techniques which included the most characteristic talud-tablero combination of a diagonal wall, built with a batter, and a vertical-section rectangular wall. The interior decoration of these edifices, the delicacy of the ceramics, the frequent use of fresco (a technique invented here) and the exquisite workmanship of the funeral masks carved from jade or basalt, all bear witness to the degree of refinement attained by the craftsmen and artists of Teotihuacan. This theocratic society worked on a pyramidal principle with, at the apex, the elite, the priest kings and their families, few in number, and, at the base, the common people. Since the kings held their authority by divine filiation, a highly structured pantheon was set in place with, as supreme deity, Quetzalcoatl, the feathered serpent. The city-state infused its culture throughout all of central Mexico and sent settlers as far afield as the lands of the Mixtecs, the Zapotecs and the Mayas to set up trading posts. By the 6th century of our era, it had become the world's sixth largest city but their sun was at its zenith.

From this time onwards, probably for a combination of climatic reasons (the lands drying out from over-intensive logging) and political factors (new city-states emerging in central Mexico), the power of Teotihuacan began to wane. In the 7th century, the city was partially destroyed by fire, perhaps voluntarily by its inhabitants for some unknown reason, before being invaded and plundered by the 'northern barbarians' - most probably the Otomis. The survivors continued some semblance of state in Atzcapotzalco but despite their efforts their civilization faded out of all existence around the year 900. The Aztecs discovered the ruins of this superb city some two centuries later and, impressed by the scale and majesty of the constructions, gave the city its name. As were all those who saw Teotihuacan, they were convinced that such a place could only have been built by gods or giants. The site continued to be regarded with respect and religious awe until the arrival of the Spanish many centuries later.

The impressive Path of the Dead,
seen here from the top of the Pyramid of the Moon, is Teotihuacan's main thoroughfare.
It is flanked on either side by palaces and the bases of sanctuaries.
The gigantic Pyramid of the Sun looms, left, in the distance.

On the upper parts of the Quetzalcoatl Temple, masks of Tlaloc, the rain god,
alternate with those of the Plumed Serpent.

Overall view of the Monte Alban site in Mexico from the northern platform.
Edifices M, L and IV may be distinguished from left to right.

The various eras of Monte Alban

The history of the Oaxaca province revolves around its three great central valleys, Tlacolula, Etla and Zimatlan. Throughout the 8th and 7th centuries BC, they were inhabited by pre-Zapotec peoples of unknown origin, strongly influenced by the Olmec culture. These original populations, newly formed from scattered tribal groups, left their mark throughout the entire Oaxaca region, notably on the worn-down site of Monte Alban, in the form of little sanctuaries, ceremonial platforms, altars, tombs and low-relief carvings. This pre-Zapotec occupation of the site is archæologically known as Monte Alban I. The Zapotec groups arrived somewhere between 300 and 200 BC, perhaps from Chiapas or from western Guatemala, and the site soon became the centre of all Oaxaca. New monuments were built during this period, referred to as Alban II, and the population of the city soared to 15,000 souls. The commoners spread their homes over the steep flanks of the site while the nobility and the priests lived in the upper city built on the flat summit. This first Zapotec culture, born of the interbreeding of the Zapotec newcomers with the original

inhabitants, was characterized by the erection of columns and massive buildings, clearly influenced by the Maya and proof of early contact between the two zones. Other waves of Zapotec migrations followed, the most numerous arriving in the early years of our era, giving rise to an astonishing cultural mix which was the foundation of the Zapotec civilization as we know it. It was to last for ten centuries and its two main periods are referred to for convenience as Monte Alban III (the high period) and Monte Alban IV (the decadence). In the course of Alban III, the city continued to grow, numbering 30,000 inhabitants who lived on artificial terraces carved out of the mountainside. The artistic influence of Teotihuacan, spread by the many trade and cultural relations between the two cities, led to the building of monuments employing the new talud-tablero technique. Monte Alban became the capital of an empire which covered the entire Oaxaca region, wielding a political influence backed by a very marked religious power over its neighbours, an authority seen in the some 200 sanctuaries the mother site governed in the surrounding district. To meet the needs of the population, a remarkable network of irrigation was built to water the rich agricultural lands surrounding the city.

Between 700 and 950, the Zapotecs gradually abandoned the Monte Alban site, certainly because of successive famines caused by the exhaustion of the agricultural resources of the central valleys.

The former empire went into an inevitable decline and, from the 12th century, came under the domination of the Mixtecs, a people originally from the Puebla-Cholula region, who ushered in the era referred to as Monte Alban V.

The famous danzantes, *stonecarvings representing wounded enemies with vaguely negroid features, have been gathered at the base of Edifice* L.

El Tajin the enigmatic

Some thirty kilometres from the shores of the Gulf of Veracruz, in a warm mountain region, stand the impressive remains of the mysterious civilization of El Tajin, so-named after the god of thunder or thunderstorms (common in this region in summer) in the Totonac language. Because of the common but misleading practice of automatically identifying sites with the tribes or peoples living there at the time of their discovery, the El Tajin civilization has often been called Totonac after the natives who populated the region when the Spanish discovered the ruins in 1785. Yet the Totonacs arrived only in the 6th century, when most of the great monuments of El Hajin were already built. We have no clear idea of their link with the original builders, of whom we know frustratingly little. Were they descendants? Or related by marriage? Or vassals? Many specialists believe that the builders were Huaxtecs, themselves related in some way to the Maya. Glottochronological analysis (a method used to calculate language divergence) has demonstrated that 3 000 years ago the Huaxtecs and the Maya spoke a common language. An original common stock may have split into two groups somewhere around 1200 BC, when the Olmec civilization was just beginning, leaving each to develop its own independent culture. It would seem that the site of El Tajin was permanently occupied from about the 1st

century AD and that the first ritual buildings were erected during the closing years of that century. Following a period of relative abandon, the city and its satellites were again fully inhabited in the late 6th century, this time by a principally Totonac population. As both trade and political capital of the Veracruz Gulf region and the religious centre of a cruel and bloodthirsty cult, the city lived its heyday between the 7th and 8th centuries, a period during which the greatest of its monuments were built, including the famous Niched Pyramid. Some experts have speculated that this curious construction once contained 364 or 365 niches and was therefore some sort of 'temple-calendar'. Most of these monuments formed a ceremonial centre dedicated to cults similar to those of Teotihuacan, a parallel which points to the probable existence of regular exchanges between the two capitals. Similarly, certain buildings in the zone called El Tajin Chico feature clearly Mayan characteristics, a further indication of the interpenetration of the various pre-Columbian civilizations. Only 150 acres of El Tajin have been cleared and excavated, a tiny proportion of a site estimated to cover ten square kilometres, lost in the middle of thick jungle. Much research has been focused on the El Tajin civilization but its tantalizing veil of mystery is still far from lifted. From the 10th century onwards, it had to struggle against several waves of barbarian invaders from the north, most probably the Chichimecs, before falling under the strong Toltec influence seen in the decoration of the ball-game courts with their scenes of decapitation and ritual sacrifices. As El Tajin slowly waned, its economic empire crumbled and its cultural influence came to an end. Towards 1200, the city was abandoned by its inhabitants. Some emigrated to the city of Zempoala to live in the company of other Totanac clans, an influx of population which boosted this community to the leadership of a sort of federation of southern Totonac states. Zempoala's influence over all this region of central Mexico continued for the next two centuries until, in the mid 15th century, it came under the control of the Aztecs.

Late Toltec influence is clearly perceptible in this detail
from a scene of human sacrifice in a ball-game court in El Tajin.

The Niched Pyramid in El Tajin (Mexico) is composed of six storeys featuring rows of niches.
The monumental stairway on the eastern facade provides access to the upper platform on which the actual temple was built.

The Mayan city-states

The Mayan territory stretched over a vast area including most or all of several southeastern Mexican states (Chiapas, Campeche, Tabasco, Yucatan and Quintana Roo), Belize, Guatemala and the western parts of El Salvador and Honduras. Nomad populations of Mayan origin roamed these lands some 2 000 years before our era and the first autochthonous cultures appeared around 1400 BC when the ancient hunter-gatherers began to settle. Between the 6th and the 4th centuries BC, a pre-Classic Mayan civilization emerged in the Pacific region and on the highlands (from Mexican Chiapas to El Salvador, including the Guatemalan altiplano). It lasted until the closing years of the 2nd century AD when, following great political and cultural upheavals, a ruling aristocracy formed, took over the military power and assumed the religious authority. Major ceremonial centres sprang up, including Izapa in the Chiapas, Kaminaljuya in Guatemala and Chalchuapa in El Salvador. A strong Olmec influence is clearly detectable in this impetus, from the famous Mayan calendar to the hieroglyphic writing, so much so that certain authors have suggested that the Mayas were distant descendants of the Olmecs. Without going this far, it must be said that a remarkable symbiosis certainly took place, across the gulf of centuries, between the two peoples.

This pre-Classic phase was followed by the Classic period, traditionally divided for convenience into the Lower Classic (200-600) and the Upper Classic (600-900). From the beginning of our era, the Mayan highlands went through bouts of decadence, brief but increasingly frequent, until, around 150, they began the period of cultural and political stagnation which led to their downfall. The focus of the Mayan world then shifted down to the forest-covered central lowlands, a slow transfer which was completed by the end of the 3rd century. On these lowlands, a new society was born, founded on a system of city-states. Pyramidal in structure, it was divided into hierarchical classes with, at the top, the ruling caste of the nobility who held the reins of political and military power together with the secrets of religious knowledge. From amongst them came a king *(halach uinic)*, the incarnation of the two supreme gods: Itzamna, son of the god of creation Hunab and master of the different skies of Night and Day, and Chac, the god of Rain, Wind and the Thunderstorm.

The slow maturation of this society was closely linked to the cultural and economic 'colonisation' of Teotihuacan towards the year 400. Incoming groups from central Mexico taught the Maya architectural techniques, such as the talud-tablero, which were new to them. They also gave them new religious elements and the Maya, who hitherto had practised their domestic cults in small-scale sanctuaries, began to construct monumental temple-pyramids in honour of a rich pantheon of great national gods. The cultural blossoming of the Classic period is conveniently marked by the setting up of stelæ which date and record the main historical and political events. Each under the iron rule of the great kings, various cities successively became the pole stars in the Mayan firmament. The first was Tikal, in the Peten forest, inhabited since the 8th century BC, which shone over the Mayan world from 230 (when the king Yax Moch Xoc came to the throne) until the year 900 (and the accession of his 26th successor, Ah Cacau). Other great centres bore witness to the splendour of the Maya. These included Palenque, in the Chiapas, which lived its finest years in the 7th century during the reigns of Pakal and his son Chan Bahlum; Yaxchilan, which knew its hour of glory in the 7th to 8th centuries during the dynasties of the Jaguar Kings; Copan, in Honduras, which, on a site inhabited for at least 1 200 years before our era, became the most important city on the eastern frontier from its official founding in the 5th century by Mah Kina Yax Kuk Mo until the beginning of the reign of its last king, U Cit Toku, in 822, and others such as Quirigua, in Guatemala, which developed its own special style in the 8th century after having escaped from the tutelage of Copan, or Xunantunich and Caracol in Belize, the latter of which counted some 150,000 inhabitants in the 7th century.

The Mayan golden age is not an exaggerated term, for each of these city-states contributed to that extraordinary intellectual and artistic movement which made the Mayan world the 'Greece of the Americas'. Yet strangely, unlike all the other regions of Central America, there was never any Mayan empire. These little kingdoms, fiercely independent, were in constant conflict with one another, the victor temporarily outstripping its rivals. This incessant internal strife was one of the factors in the Mayan decline in the 8th century, but not the only one. The region was also ravaged by natural catastrophes which included epidemics, floods followed by droughts which impoverished the land and led to famines, earthquakes, hurricanes... The political situation became more and more unstable. The ruling caste of

Temple 1 or the Temple of the Jaguars in Tikal (Guatemala) is one of the finest expressions of classic Mayan art.
It was built over a royal tomb in the 8th century AD.

nobility seemed progressively alienated from the people, peasants' revolts broke out on several occasions and the priest-astronomers, convinced that their universe was destined to fall because of the alternating cycle of periods of glory and darkness, abandoned ship, leaving the society rudderless without its spiritual guides.

Despite its genius and in spite of its remarkable powers of self-renewal, the Mayan world was unable to survive. Its programmed end was predictable; the Mayans themselves had given the date - the end of the 18th katum of the 9th *baktun* - in our terms, the year 790. And thus the brilliant civilization of the central lowlands began its slow death. The stelæ, signs of good health, were no longer erected: in 801 in Copan, in 807 in Yaxchilan, in 810 in Edzna, Piedras Negras and Quirigua, in 849 in Oxkintok, in 869 in Tikal and in 889 in Jimbal, Xultun, Xamantun...

Another Mayan civilization was to take over further north, but it was no longer the purely Mayan creation of this first period.

The Classic period saw the blossoming of many prosperous city-states. The most famous of these were Tikal (rear photo showing the summits of temple-pyramids standing out from the forest) and Uaxactum (Structure E VII) in Guatemala, Yaxchilan (Structure 33 with its high openwork roof crest) in Mexico and Copán (head of the Spectators' Tribune) in Honduras.

Overall view of the Tulum site in Mexico.
The buildings, small and poorly built, are characteristic of the closing years of the post-Classic Mayan period.

The kingdoms and military empires of the post-Classic

All the great Classic civilizations
came to an end before the close of the first millenary,
victims of their own decline but also of the invasions
of the Chichimecs, the generic term applied by the
Anahuac peoples to the tribes
of northern barbarians.
The post-Classic was a period of almost constant
warfare and strife, characterized by the appearance
of military architecture and regulated
by the struggle for power.

The Toltec model

The Chichimecs ('Red heads' or 'Born of dogs') were a nomad people who had been pushing up against the northern frontiers of the great central Mexican states for several centuries and who flooded through the weak point left by the declining civilizations. One of these peoples, the Toltec, established a small empire whose far-reaching influence changed the entire Anahuac. Literally idolized by their successors, they began by peacefully uniting central Mexico after the fall of Teotihuacan. Their military and religious system then took a cruel turn which was to contaminate most of the following cultures and civilizations down into Nicaragua and, for some, even as far as Costa Rica. Legend has it that they shifted from a semi-theocratic state to a kingdom ruled by warrior princes. According to two codices, Tula, thought to be their capital from the 10th century onwards, was originally governed by a succession of ten semi-mythical kings who reigned from 856 (date of the founding of Tula) to 1168 (the date of its destruction by other Chichimec tribes), a 312-year period which neatly formed six cycles or ritual Mesoamerican centuries of 52 years. The

most important figure in this dynasty was Ce Acatl Topiltzin, who ruled as Quetzalcoatl, a name borrowed from the new deity dominant in central Mexico since the fall of Teotihuacan. Quetzalcoatl, the lord of Wind and of Life, was the son of the celestial god Mixcoatl and the earthly goddess Chimalman. He had come down to earth to bring men agriculture, the calendar, architecture, painting, writing and other achievements, but a god from the north, Tezcatlipoca, the sovereign of Night, the Moon and the Stars and a power associated with thieves and brigands, had driven him out and replaced him with Huémac, the divinity who introduced the practices of human sacrifices, of ritual wars to provide victims, of the ball games which frequently ended with the execution of the losers... Under his impulsion, the Toltec society became steeped in blood and infused with the culture of warfare. Quetzalcoatl fled to the east where he transformed himself into the Morning Star after prophesying his own return.

Many years later, a certain Cortes was to turn this myth to his advantage, using it to bolster the Indians' belief in the divine nature of the Spanish.

The Toltec and the Teotihuacan cultures had so many points of similarity that it was long believed that the latter was the religious capital and Tula the administrative capital of one and the same empire. It is now established that, through groups of emigrants (probably the Nonoalcas, who fled the destruction of Teotihuacan in the 7th century), the Toltecs were in fact the first inheritors of the prestigious city-states. They very quickly set their own imprint on their inheritance. Whereas the Teotihuacan religion worshipped a complex pantheon, the Tulan system was much more monotheistic, with Quetzalcoatl as its

The upper platform of Tlahuizcalpantecuhtli ('Morning Star') in Tula (Mexico) features four basalt telamones and pillars which once supported the sanctuary roof. The Indians still come here sometimes to pay homage to the ancient gods.

central pillar. Similarly, the hitherto ruling class of priests was replaced in the social pyramid by the institution of a single king, son of the gods, vested with the triple powers of state - political, military and religious - and supported by a caste of ennobled warriors from his own clan. The Toltec empire, under the ferule of the pitiless god Tezcatlipoca, became a veritable reign of blood and war from the 11th century onwards, paradoxically the most remarkable culture of its time. For almost two centuries, while its armies and its traders travelled Mesoamerica from central Mexico to the Mayan lands, the religious and civilizing influence of Tula was such that all the later Mexican dynasties were to claim Toltec descent. Just as the founders of Chichen Itza in the Yucatan were Toltec emigrants, the Toltec contribution to the Phurepecha, Aztec and Mixtec cultures was fundamental. Some specialists have even suggested links with the Chorotegas in Nicaragua.

Whatever their importance, the arrogant power of the Toltecs began to crumble towards the late 12th century and was unable to withstand the onslaught of new Chichimec tribes who took Tula in the early years of the 12th century and destroyed it in 1168. The survivors scattered over Central America, often to influence local cultures throughout the continent.

Aztecs, Tarascans and Mixtecs

In the course of the 13th and 14th centuries, two peoples from the north began to settle on new lands further south, one on the shores of Lake Texcoco in the Mexico City valley, the other around Lake Patzcuara in the present state of Michoacan. The first were the Mexicas ('Sons of Mexitl'), one of the Teochichimec (literally 'real Chichimec') nomad tribes, speaking the Nahuatl language of their group. The name of the second people remains a mystery; they have been called Tarascan since the 16th century, when the Spanish conquistadores, thinking that they heard the word 'tarasco' often repeated in the native language, took it for their name. Although the Aztecs considered the Tarascans to be real Chichimecs, it would seem they were of different stock, yet unknown, which, having long lived in close proximity with the Chichimecs, adopted their customs down through the passage of time.

According to tradition, the Mexicas originated from the region of the Seven Caves, called Chicomozoc, from which came the seven original Chichimec tribes who each founded a state in one of the valleys of Mexico; the Acolhuas in Texcoco, the Chalcas in Chalco, the Colhuas in Culhuacan, the Tlahuicas in Cuernavaca, the Tlatepotzcas in Huejotzingo and Tlaxcala, the Chinampanecas in Xochimilco and the Tepanecas in San Angel. The Aztecs, while affirming their close kinship with these seven tribes, situated their own homeland in Aztlan (possibly in the state known as Nayarit today), whence they derived their name. According to their codices, they began their migration south in 1168, the very year of the fall of Tula, led by their mythical king Xolot I, himself inspired by the sun god of war Mexitl, better known as Huitzilopochtli. Local populations along their route, already settled, received these barbarians with cold stares. Only Coxcox, the Toltec soveriegn of Colhuacan, seems to have allowed them to camp on his lands, *cont. page 91*

Details of the decorative work on the side stonework of Tlahuizcalpantecuhtli.
The reliefs show prowling pumas and jaguars and eagles devouring human hearts.

*This carved rock
showing an Aztec shield is set
before the entrance to the
Cortes Palace
in Cuernavaca in Mexico.
It belonged to the ancient pyramid
the conquistador had destroyed
to make way for his palace.*

*The religious centre of Xochicalco ('Place of the House of Flowers') in Mexico was occupied,
successively, by the Olmecs, the Toltecs, the Maya, the Zapotecs, the Mixtecs and the Aztecs. The best-known monument,
the Pyramid of the Plumed Serpent, was perhaps built for a very important meeting of astronomer-priests.*

The conquistadores left few Aztec monuments standing in Mexico.
Some remarkable remains can still be seen, however, like the circular temple of Malinalco with its jaguar and eagle heads,
the Tenayuca pyramid with its long flights of stairs and the serpent-decorated base of the Major Temple in Teocalli.

The city of Tzintzuntzan ('Place of the Hummingbirds') in Mexico,
built on a hillock east of lake Patzcuaro, was the capital of the Tarasque empire.
The principal remains include the bases of five yacatas or temples,
built from flat stones piled in layers and held in place by the slope of the walls.

Mitla, in the Mexican Oaxaca,
is a perfect example of urban Zapotec architecture 'corrected' by the Mixtecs.

on condition that they help him combat his rivals. The Aztecs showed their prowess, proving themselves extremely useful allies, and Coxcox decided to give his daughter in marriage to the Aztec chief, Nopaltzin, who, mistakenly and unfortunately, sought to honour her by sacrificing her to his gods! Immediately driven away in disgrace, the Aztecs continued their migration southwards, seeking the spot where they were to found their capital, a spot which, according to prophecy, would be marked by an eagle, perched on a prickly pear, devouring a snake. They found it, somewhere between 1325 and 1345, on the shores of Lake Texcoco, a site already occupied by several peoples: the descendants of the original Chichimec groups (notably the Tepanecas) and the Toltecs who had fled the fall of Tula. The Aztecs founded a city which they called Tenochtitlan (possibly from "city of Tenoch", in remembrance of the high priest who had guided the migration of their people). The first houses were built on a marshy and particularly unhealthy part of the lagoon, the only site where the Tepanec king of Atzcapotzalco had allowed them to settle. After first having hired themselves as mercenaries, they rose against the Tepanecas in 1427, led by their fourth king Itzcoatl, who took the title of *tlatoani* or 'he who speaks'. With this victory, the Aztecs were now masters of the valley. In 1429, two years after their putsch, Itzcoatl concluded a triple pact with the neighbouring cities of Tlacopan and Texcoco. This confereration allowed the Aztec nation, leader in the coalition, to head a vast military empire which soon occupied all of central Mexico right up to the base of the Yucatan. Tenochtitlan became a powerful city whose society was founded on a very rigid code of laws and moral rules laid down mostly by Tlacælel, one of the most important Aztec high priests, a dignitary who had survived four kings. He had all the books and codices of the conquered peoples burned, instituted the myth of the chosen people, the Sons of the Sun, heirs of the Toltec, and had Montezuma I declare the "flowering war" (*xochig aogotl*) which justified any military action, even in time of peace, to obtain victims for the gods. In the 16th century, when the Spanish took Tenochtitlan, they discovered an immense city of over half a million inhabitants. Temples and magnificent palaces, built on artificial foundations, lined the innumerable streets and canals. All the conquistadors' accounts agree on one point; they had the impression of arriving in a new Venice! Tragically, everything was destroyed in 1521 and Cuauhtemoc, the last Aztec ruler, was executed four years later.

In their struggle for domination of central Mexico, the Aztecs ran up against the empire the Tarascans had created from Lake Patzcuaro to the Pacific. Also called the Phurepechas, after the Indian tribes who later descended from them, this people spoke a language unlike any of their neighbours' and we have no idea what they called themselves. Arriving, most probably, in Michoacan somewhere around the late 13th to early 14th century, they interbred with a Chichimec people yet still preserved many of their own customs (pottery and woodworking, advanced agricultural techniques...). In the late 14th century, Tariacuri, one of the kings of Tzintzuntzan, founded the Tarascan league with the two cities of Patzcuaro and Ihuatzio. Upon his death, his successors extended the kingdom into an empire, progressively engulfing the rival kingdoms of Zacatollan, Coliman, Zapotlan, Jalisco and Tonalan. The Tarascan power long matched that of the much-feared Aztecs who, despite many campaigns in the course of the 15th century, never managed to defeat these rivals. In the early days of the following century, however, the Spanish soldiers, under Nuno de Guzman, a leader of legendary cruelty, put a definitive end to the Tarascan civilization, drowning it in blood.

In the Oaxaca, the Mixtecs, originally from the highlands of the present state (despite the ancient tradition which has them belonging to the seven tribes of Chicomoztoc), had replaced the Zapotecs by the 10th century, ousting them by three centuries of incessant warfare and through interbreeding. Skilled potters and renowned ironsmiths, the Mextecs also produced superb jewellery and gold masks. They were divided into three allied kingdoms, Coixtlahuaca in the North (founded, it is said, by Toltec emigrants), Achiutla in the centre and Tutotepec in the South. Under the influence of the Toltecs, their society took a decidedly military turn and human sacrifices, ball games and ritual wars became commonplace.

Throughout the 15th century, they defended their territory tooth and nail against the Aztec armies sent against them successively by the *tlatoanis* Montezuma I and Axayacatl, but had to bow to the power of their attackers in the early 16th century.

Many rebellions followed, but they were never able to shake off the Aztec yoke and remained in thrall until the arrival of the Spaniards, against whom they again put up a doughty resistance. Cortez finally subjugated them definitively in 1527 during his expedition south to Guatemala.

The Toltec-Mayas of the Yucatan

As we saw above, Toltec groups emigated towards other horizons after the fall of Tula in the 13th century, and it is now confirmed that one of them drifted as far as the Yucatan. At this time, the Mayan world was in the throes of an unprecedented crisis which had begun in the 9th century. The brilliant city-states of the Classic period were falling into disrepair and the jungle had already claimed many of the monuments. According to the codices, warriors led by a certain Kukulcan (literal translation of Quetzalcoatl, the feathered serpent, in the Itza language) had conquered the northern part of the Yucatan towards the end of

These two monumental serpentine columns, clearly of Toltec influence,
once supported the roof of the entrance to the Warriors' Temple in Chichen Itza in Mexico.

the 10th century. The Mayas baptised these new arrivals the Itzas, or "those who speak our language badly". These Itzas founded their capital next to a cenote, one of those deep sinkholes in the limestone of the peninsula, declaring it sacred - hence its name Chichen Itza, or "the well of the Itzas". The site had been inhabited by the Mayas since 550, but abandoned towards the year 900 for reasons which remain obscure, before being repopulated by other Mayas in the late 10th century. It would seem that the Itzas were the result of interbreeding between the Toltec exiles and the local populations and indeed the cultural simi-larities between Tula and Chichen Itza are striking. The Kukulkan and the Toltec Quelzalcoatl shared a

General view of the Warriors' Temple. To the right of the central sanctuary can be seen part of the Group of 1000 Columns,
a series of porticoes which mark off a rectangular area made up of meeting rooms.

common emblem, the eagle-jaguar. The Warriors' Temple of Chichen Itza and Structure B in Tula were built along identical architectural lines. Both cities contained flat-roofed houses supported by beams and masonry, quite unlike the traditional Mayan houses with their corbel or 'false' vaults, and the list of other Toltec architectural elements in the Itzan city includes the feline friezes, the snail-shaped crenellations, the altars supported by telamons, the celebrated *chac-mools* and many others. On a perhaps less cultural level, the Toltec influence was further seen in the systematic practice of human sacrifices and ritual wars.

The Governor's Palace in Uxmal (Mexico), preceded by a little structure bearing a sacrificial chac mool, boasts a remarkable facade, 300 feet long, decorated in the purest Puuc style.

The neighbouring Mayans also left their cultural imprint on the Itzas. The priestly class was adopted and the Mayan pantheon (notably the god Chac) included into the Toltec religious patrimony. This civilization should thus really be referred to as syncretic, created from a mixing of Toltec-influenced Mayas and Mayan-influenced Toltecs. Chichen Itza ruled undisputed over the lowlands until the late 12th century, fuelling the cultural renaissance of the whole region, a movement which also benefited cities such as Uxmal and Mayapan. Founded, according to legend, by Kukulkan in 1007, this latter city was governed by the dynasty of the Cocomes, a people originally from Mexico and related to the Itzas. They organized a confederation of the main city-states on the Yucatan, composed principally of Chichen Itza, Uxmal and Izamal, but subsequent rivalries between the Itzas and the Cocomes put an end to this so-called Mayapan league and Uxmal and Izamal became simply satellites of Mayapan. The Cocomes grew strong enough to

attack and pillage Chichen Itza towards the end of the 12th century and the once-proud capital of the Itzas was abandoned. Some of its chieftains managed to escape to Tayasal, on the shores of Lake Peten, where they organized a little kingdom. Soon Mayapan, as the capital of great and pitiless sovereigns such as Hunac Ceel Canuch, was propelled to the head of a full-scale empire which exerted its military rule over the entire northern part of the Yucatan peninsula (over 30,000 km²) for almost two and a half centuries. This domination came to an end in 1460 when Ah Xupan Tutul Xiu, one of the kings of Uxmal (a territory governed since the early 11th century by the Xius dynasty who had come from the Mexican Anahuac in the footsteps of the Kukulkan), led a general rebellion and overthrew the Cocomes oppressors, razing Mayapan to the ground. The Xius of Uxmal attempted to take control over the region but the Cocomes empire fragmented into a score of little squabbling states which proved ungovernable. The Yucatan slid into a long period of anarchy which lasted until the arrival of the Montejo conquistadors in the 16th century. The Mayan cities fell, one after the other, to the Europeans and only the Itzas of Tayasal were able to hold off the Spanish advances until 1697.

From the top of the Nuns' Edifice in Chichen Itza, the view extends to the Caracol or 'Snail' observatory,
so-called because of its shape, with, in the background, the lofty pyramidal form of Castillo.

Paquimés and Chorotegas

Each in its own limited sphere, other more modest cultures attempted to thrive in the shade of the 'heavyweight' civilizations we have just seen. Two of these merit special mention, qualifying as civilizations as much because of their politico-social organization and their artistic inventiveness as because of their cultural influence over the region surrounding them: those of the Paquimé in northern Mexico and of the Chorotega in Nicaragua.

To the west of the town of Casas Grandes, in the state of Chihuahua, a collection of remarkable ruins speak of the former presence of a major population centre dating back to the Classic period, probably a part of the cultural group known as the 'American Oasis'. Between the beginning of our era and the year 900, various cultures blossomed in this region which extends from the southwest of the United States (Arizona, New Mexico, Colorado and Utah) over into the northwest of Mexico (Sonora and Chihuahua). Isolated in the

middle of the American desert, this zone had no contact with the rest of Mesoamerica, notably the Anahuac plateau, until the 10th century. It thus developed its own particular way, best illustrated by the cultures of the Hokokam, the Mogollon and the Anasazi.

In the early 10th century, far-reaching political upheavals shook the American Oasis. For reasons still not fully understood, some of the peoples moved up to the northwest whereas others began a long march south. As the formerly distinct cultures were diluted and mixed with one another, some disappeared and others were enriched. It would seem that the civilization of the Paquimé, also called the civilization of the Casas Grandes, was born of a fusion between the Hokokam-Mogollon-Anasazi groups. From the middle of the 10th century to the 14th, the Paquimé merchants controlled all the trade in northern Mexico. Their territory was dotted with trading posts and warehouses and criss-crossed with a network of carefully tended trails. Their agriculture flourished and they had developed various types of stockbreeding. Their craftsmen had perfected techniques for working stone (notably a green variety which, once polished, provided magnificent costume ornaments), copper, mother of pearl (imported from the Pacific), bone and other raw materials. Their potters were famous, creating first monochromatic work and, latterly, black or red or white ware, decorated with geometric or stylised patterns, and their capital, whose real name remains undiscovered and which we call Paquimé after the natives who inhabited the region, is a magnificent example of a fortified adobe city. Today we can admire the partly restored ruins of the ramparts, the little pyramids, the

Some of the anthropomorphic objects from the Casas Grandes ('Big Houses') civilization, found during excavations at Paquimé.

ball courts and, particularly, the blocks of houses, often oblong and two or three storeys high, which lined the streets and were furnished with water supplies. Some are even equipped with an astonishing collective heating system. Their narrow I-shaped doors and windows are highly reminiscent of those of the Pueblo Indians of the southwestern United States. The Paquimé civilization came to a sudden end in 1340 when the capital was invaded and burned by people from the north, most probably Apaches.

Many testimonials point to ancient human presence in western Nicaragua, notably the Acahualinca footprints. A group of our early ancestors, men, women and children, left their tracks in the ash which was to bury them alive in the course of a volcanic eruption - no doubt Mount Masaya - some 6000 years ago. Various Indian peoples lived in the region between the lakes and the Pacific shoreline. Of these, the

Overall view of the great adobe city of Paquimé.
Flourishing trade made it the economic capital of northern Mexico for three centuries.

The Paquimé city planners were masters of the art of adobe building and water channelling.
Characteristic I-shaped doors were a standard feature of every house and buildings of one to three storeys were built on beams let into the walls.

Chorotega gained the upper hand over the others in the late 9th century and went on to develop an original form of society based on a hierarchy of castes and a well-filled pantheon. In the years between 1000 and 1200, their civilization underwent a second phase of development, perhaps influenced by Nahuatl-speaking Mexican peoples. The neighbours of the Chorotega, the Nicaraos, were, after all,

directly descended from groups who had emigrated from central Mexico. Under this new inspiration, a monumental style of statuary began to appear. Huge basalt sculptures have been found by the shores of Lake Nicaragua and on the islands of Zapatera and Omotepe (literally "between two hills" in Nahuatl), generally representing 'double beings' composed of men, often warriors, to which an animal is 'attached', either decoratively (like the costumes of the Aztec warrior-eagles or warrior-jaguars) or symbolically (the protective spirit of an individual taking the form of a totem animal). In the 13th century, for reasons still unfathomed, this civilization literally dissipated, gradually letting its brilliance and its influence soak into the sands like water from an overturned bottle. When the Spanish arrived two centuries later, many of the Chorotegas had lost all remembrance of their glorious past and become mere vassals of the Nicaraos, the people who gave their name to the country.

The Chorotegas of Nicaragua created the most astonishing statues in Central America, representing half-human, half-animal mythological beings and strangely deformed personages.

3
The people of four cultures

Today's inhabitants of Central America are divided into four communities: Indian, white, mixed-blood and black. The mixed-bloods may represent the largest portion of the population, but political and economic power is still mostly concentrated in the hands of the white élite. The Indians, bludgeoned by five centuries of colonialism, have retreated into a defensive silence while the blacks, last on the social scale, are turning to other horizons.

◁ *A Lacandon family. This tribe, originally from the Mexican southern Yucatán and the Guatemalan Peten, arrived in the Chiapas in the course of the 18th century. Their name probably derives from Acam Tun, an island on Lake Miramar near which they settled.*

The silence of the Indians

The first inhabitants
of the region, the Amerindians,
first underwent the traumatic process of the
Conquest before being subjected to colonization,
a cultural steamroller which attempted
to crush their traditional structures.
The Central American countries may now have
attained independence, but the Indians' living
conditions have changed little.
Often considered as second-class citizens,
they seem to watch History go past
with indifference.

*In the Emberas tribe in Panama, the heads of families discuss the question at length in the 'council room'
before taking any decision on matters affecting the community.*

The temptation of isolation

The Mesoamerican Indians of today form a heterogeneous group of some 35 million individuals distributed as follows : 27,200,000 in Mexico (29% of the overall population), 5,700,000 in Guatemala (54%), 22,000 in Belize (10%), 425,000 in Honduras (7%), 540,000 in El Salvador (9%), 132,000 in Nicaragua (3%), 35,000 in Costa Rica (1%) and 168,000 in Panama (6%). Simply looking at the raw figures, we can see that the Indian population of Central America is in poor shape, very often cut off from modern society. Those who dominated the subcontinent five centuries ago now only represent 26% of the total population. Long considered as inferiors and excluded from the white and half-caste society, the Indians held their heads high again in the closing years of the 19th century when the great half-caste revolutionary movements broke out. They should then have taken the place by right theirs in the new society but despite the real or pretended efforts of the governments who successively managed the affairs of the various

Mesoamerican states, they have become more and more marginalized, often indeed through their own doing, and have taken refuge in a silence which may be sometimes haughty but is always sad. The result today is an incredible patchwork of ethnic Indian groups which, cut off from one another, have no political weight. The only exceptions in this sea of silence are the Tzotzils and the Tzeltals in Mexico and the Cunas in Panama, tribes who have joined the vocal pan-Indian movements demanding recognition of the Amerindian cultures and advocating a return to ancestral values such as the extended family, the worship of the dead and the forces of Nature, the traditional structure of society... Mexico alone numbers 92 different indigenous languages, not to speak of the innumerable dialects, and in the state of Oaxaca alone, researchers have counted no less than 66 distinct ethnic groups. The Indians in Guatemala are almost all Maya, yet they speak 28 languages, divided into nine major families, whose speakers cannot understand one another!

Despite the extreme fragmentation of the communities, it is interesting to draw up a panorama of the main ethnic Indian groups in Central America. This comprehensive presentation includes all the best-known groups in each country and the figures are those from the most recent census and available official estimates (some of these figures may be deliberately underestimated by the authorities and most, as is standard practice in Latin America, do not include children under the age of five).

Initiation ceremonies are commonplace among the Tarahumaras in the Mexican Chihuahua.
The exact details of each are carefully settled by a council made up of shamans and temporal chieftains.

*This young mother and her son are among the last of the Bribris living
on the Caribbean coast of Costa Rica.*

MEXICO

Total Indian population estimated at 27,200,000 individuals, of whom nine and a half million are considered pure-blooded, divided into various ethnic groups, the main being as follows:

Ethnic group	Number	Locality
Yaquis	23 500	state of Sonora
Tarahumaras	72 000	state of Chihuahua
Coras	16 900	state of Nayarit
Tepehuans	24 700	state of Durango
Huichols	25 400	state of Jalisco and Nayarit
Mayos	48 800	state of Sonora
Huaxtecas	58 000	states of San Luis Potosi and Veracruz
Phurepechas	205 000	state of Michoacan
Otomis	375 400	states of Hidalgo and Mexico
Mazahuas	173 500	state of Mexico
Nahuas	1 620 000	states of Mexico, Veracruz, and Puebla
Popolocas	41 600	state of Veracruz
Totonacas	265 000	state of Veracruz
Tlapanecas	95 000	state of Guerrero
Amuzgos	37 700	states of Guerrero and Oaxaca
Cuicatecas	39 000	states of Guerrero and Oaxaca
Zapotecas	630 000	state of Oaxaca
Mixtecas	510 000	state of Oaxaca
Triques	6 800	state of Oaxaca
Chinantecas	1 430 000	state of Oaxaca
Mazatecas	208 000	state of Oaxaca
Tequistlatecas	24 300	state of Oaxaca
Mixes	124 800	state of Oaxaca
Chatinos	38 500	state of Oaxaca
Zoques	56 300	state of Chiapas
non-Yucatan Mayas	875 000	states of Chiapas and Tabasco
Yucatan Mayas	810 000	states of Chiapas and Quintana Roo

Also featured in this list must be the ethnic groups which may be statistically tiny today but whose cultural or political influence was once far-reaching. These include the 900 Seris, the 2 500 Opatas and the 3 000 Pimas, all living in the Sonora, and the 500 Lacandons who are slowly disappearing in the Chiapas forests.

BELIZE

Overall Indian population put at 22,200, divided into various ethnic groups, most of which are Mayan:

Yucatan Mayas	8 000	district of Corozal
non-Yucatan Mayas	10 500	Belize and Cayo districts

GUATEMALA

Total Indian population estimated at 5,700,000, again divided into a host of ethnic groups, almost all within the Mayan family:

Yucatan Mayas	40 000	county of Peten
non-Yucatan Mayas	5 650 000	counties of Izabal, Alta Verapaz, Baja Verapaz, Escuintla, Guatemala, Jutiapa, Chiquimula, Zacapa, Quiché, Solola, Totonicapan, Mazatenango, Quetzaltenango, Huehuetenango

SALVADOR

Overall Indian population reckoned at 540,000 individuals spread among various ethnic groups with small populations in each. The main groups are the Xincas, descendants of the last Pipils, and the related Izalcos and Panchos. Almost all these Indians live in the mountains in the southwest of the country (counties of Achuachapan, Santa Ana and Sonsonate).

HONDURAS

Total Indian population estimated at 425,000, again spread over different, very small ethnic groups. The main tribes are as follows:

Chortis Mayas	4 500	counties of Copan and Santa Barbara
Miskitos	38 000	countries of Colon and Gracias a Dios
Lencas	100 000	county of Lempira
Tolupans (or Jicaques)	11 500	county of Yoro
Tawahkas (or Sumos)	4 000	county of Gracias a Dios
Pechs (or Payas)	2 800	county of Gracias a Dios

NICARAGUA

Estimated at 132,000, this overall Indian population is distributed among various, very small ethnic groups as follows:

Nicaraos (very integrated)	80 000	counties of Leon, Managua, and Masaya
Miskitos	33 000	all the Caribbean coast, notably the county of Zelaya
Tawahkas (ou Sumos)	3 000	Rio San Juan
Ramas	2 500	

COSTA RICA

Total Indian population estimated at 35,000, divided amongst various ethnic groups, each, in itself, quite tiny. The main groups are the Bribris, the Borucas, the Cabecars, the Terrabas and the Guatusos. Most of these Indians live in the highlands bordering the Atlantic and the Caribbean coasts (notably the province of Limon) and in certain parts of the Western Cordillera (province of Guanacaste).

PANAMA

Overall Indian population reckoned to be 168,000, spread over various ethnic groups, many of which are small :

Cunas	37 000	territory of (Comarca) de San Blas
Guaymis	82 000	provinces of Bocas del Toro, de Chiriqui, and Veraguas
Ngobés-Buglés	11 000	provinces of Chiriqui and David
Chocos-Emberas	3 600	provinces of Panama and Darien.

Other tiny groups, such as the Teribes and the Bokotas, who still survive in the provinces of Bocas del Toro and Chiriqui, should also be added to complete this picture.

During the important ceremony of the 'first corncobs', the Huichols of the Mexican Sierra de Berberia lay the first fruits of the harvest on the altars or in niches facing east so that the first rays of the sun can 'bless' the grain.

A group of Tarasques boating to Patzcuara market (Mexico) on a fine winter morning.
These two young women belong to the Chocos group,
a collective name which covers several of the Darien tribes in Panama.

Wisdom speaks in the features of this Honduran Lenca. His tribe lives in the isolated western mountain ranges.
Despite efforts to assimilate them, the El Salvadoran Indians have preserved most of their customs,
notably the costumes such as that worn by this old Pipil lady from Nahuizalco.

The Indian Front

There have always been Indian rebellions. One preconceived idea that should be punctured here is the notion (no doubt fostered by the colonial authorities) that the Indians took their defeat by the European tamely. The truth is quite the opposite; from the very beginnings of the colonization, the local peoples never accepted that might was right. In the mid-16th century there were major popular uprisings. Two of the most celebrated took place in Honduras and in Mexico. In 1537, Lempira, the emblematic chieftain of the Honduran Lencas, threw 30,000 warriors against the Spanish and forced them to withdraw from his territory. A year later, invited to come and sign a peace treaty, he was taken in an ambush and treacherously assassinated. As a sign of atonement, his name has been given to the present Honduran national currency.

In 1541-1542, the Mixton War bloodied the state of Zacatecas in Mexico. The Cascan tribes of Tlaltenango, Nochistlan, Jalpa and Juchipila rose against the invaders, torching the churches and slaughtering the colonists and Christian priests. The fires of rebellion spread and set alight all the mountains of the region. Flushed with their initial successes, the Indians ventured down to attack the towns, all defended by strong Spanish garrisons, before setting siege to the great city of Guadalajara. But the firepower of the European soldiers won the day. The viceroy Mendoza pursued the rebels back into their mountain fastnesses and put a bloody end to their revolt, terminating what historians term the "second conquest of Mexico". Crushed time and time again, the Indian resistance always managed to stagger back to its feet and its representatives participated in all the major rebellions which allowed them to reaffirm an identity so often erased by the colonial power, especially in the 19th and early 20th centuries. 1968 was the year of the Indian reawakening. Impelled by a sweeping Amerindian movement generated by the rapprochement of the different militant ethnic groups in North America (the Sioux, Cheyenne, Comanche, Navajos and others), Central America (the Tzotil, Huichol, Cuna...) and South America (the Guambiano, Aymara, Mapuche...), a real Indian Front took form, demanding recognition of the specifically Amerindian culture and advocating the return to certain pre-Columbian values. Taken lightly at first by the governments in power at the time,

The Miskitos live on the Caribbean coast in the so-called 'Mosquito region' of Honduras and Nicaragua.
A father and his son take advantage of the falling dusk, the best time of day, to fish in the marshlands bordering the mangroves.

the movement subsequently gained weight and impetus and has won considerable concessions such as autonomy for certain regions with a high Indian population. It is interesting to note that many métis, long rejected by the white community (and other métis with an overly high proportion of Indian blood), have now joined forces with the Indians and are among the most militant defenders of the cause. The Ladino

phenomenon in Guatemala is particularly telling in that the term 'Ladino' covers a whole sector of the urban population, composed of some pure-blood Indians but mostly of mixed-bloods who, having chosen the European way of life, found themselves rejected by the white population and who therefore, stalemated by ostracism, have now decided to change camps and fight for their Amerindian roots.

The Indian associations now enjoy high media coverage. Their actions are either pacifist, like the 1979 movement which gave birth to the A.N.I.S. (National El Salvadoran Native Association) or the 1981 process which generated the T.I.C.M. (Toledo Indian Culture Movement) to defend the Mopans in Belize, or militant, where no other solution seems possible, such as the Zapatist rebellion in the Chiapas or the struggle pitting the Tzotil and Tzeltal against the Mexican government since 1994, a fight for freedom which we shall examine more closely in chaper 20 below.

These two children from the Coras group in the Mexican Sierra de Nayar are busy making a bow.
Intimidated by the presence of a stranger, they have prudently come to sit in front of the family house.

The colonial architecture of Central America is a harmonious adaptation of European concepts to local conditions,
a happy marriage which produces flowing lines and a wealth of colours.

The colonial imprint

Seen through the intervening centuries,
we now imagine that the Spanish conquered
and then massively colonized the New World.
But the true story was, in fact, quite different.
The first half of the 16th century saw fewer than
7 000 conquistadors disembark in South America.
In the closing years of that same century,
some 3 000 permanent European residents
colonized lands containing a total population
of 25 million natives.

A social elite attached to its privileges

Despite its very limited numbers, the white community managed to implement a social pyramid which enthroned them at the summit of the social scale. The members of this aristocracy were of course the Spanish born back in the home country, who were called Europeans or *Gachupins* or *Chapetons*, and the Creoles (also called the Spaniards), who were the whites born on the American continent. Even throughout the 17th and 18th centuries, when the colonization programme was at its height, the white population, of *Gachupins* and Creoles alike, remained low. The New World had never really attracted either the Spanish nobility or, and which was much more serious, the Iberian womenfolk. This lack of appeal (and ladies) meant that, from the second or third generation onwards, the number of whites of pure European stock began to level out or even to diminish. The proud rivalry between the Europeans and the Creoles was one of the ineluctable features of Central American life. It led to the great rebellions of the late 19th century and began when the Europeans, freshly off the ships from Spain, had to suffer humiliations from the rich Creoles who saw the country of their birth as their property. The newcomers had only the purity of their Iberian blood to boast of and they had no hesitation in doing so. Thus the two communities found themselves in two opposing camps with, on the one hand, the rich Creoles, considered as 'half-whites' by their rivals, and, on the other, the 'true white' Europeans who claimed the political power. The Creoles, despite their antagonistic position, nevertheless set great store on marriage with Europeans, considering that this alliance with Old World blood brought them a Spanish legitimacy which has always been a sign of respectability in Latin America.

This same desire for legitimacy also inspired the marriages made, at least in the early days of the conquest and colonization, with the families from the Indian nobility. Those of Cortes and Alvarado with Indian princesses illustrate that need to give a legal backing to their lineage which prevailed throughout the entire 16th century. The frequency of these marriages alarmed the state supervisory authorities to such an extent that they took the decision to create the famous caste system in the beginning of the 17th century, classifying individuals according to the purity of their blood and, thus, the colour of their skin. A socio-racial table was therefore drawn up, with whites at the top, Indians in the middle and half-castes at the bottom, and made official. This caste system did not last out the century but, although the law may have changed, the way of thinking did not and the whites kept their absolute primacy despite the fact that their proportion of the overall population continued to diminish regularly with regard to the other bloodlines. It should be noted that many of the whites showed great and active concern about the fate of the Indians and that the Spanish Crown itself always tried to make sure that the elementary rights of its new subjects were respected. A royal edict, for example, inspired by a papal recommendation, decreed that "any infidel, once converted and baptised, must be immediately freed of human bondage". A royal proclamation of 1542 stated that "from this day onwards, whether in situation of war or in any other circumstances, even in the case of rebellion, we hereby order and demand that the Indians be treated as subjects of the Crown of Castile, as indeed they are". These fine words and fine intentions were, alas, often ignored by the *encomenderos*, those great landowners to whom the law 'entrusted' natives to have them civilized and put to work, and by a corrupt colonial civil service which magnified social differences to the benefit of the white class.

The internal rivalries and struggles between the whites of Spanish origin and those born in Mesoamerica have long disappeared. Yet 'racial purity' still remains an important factor for social ranking in Central America. Even though most of the present-day white families have some proportion of native blood, their members continue to loudly proclaim themselves 'purebloods'.

The white community in Central America is reckoned at around 18,700,000, in other terms less than 14% of the total population. The size of this white segment (including those claiming pure European ancestry) varies greatly according to the various states. They account for practically 85% of the Costa Rican population but only 17% of the Nicaraguan, 15% of the Mexican, 10% of the Panamanian, 4% of the Belizean, 1.3% of the Honduran and a tiny 1% of the El Salvadoran. Most of the presidents and high-ranking state officials in the Mesoamerican states are elected and selected from among these white communities. And even when they do not exercise power directly, the whites have sufficient influence or represent such powerful lobbies that they generally have some indirect hand in the affairs of state.

The Casa de los Azulejos, built in 1596 in Mexico,
is a magnificent example of Mudejar architecture.
The facade is decorated with ceramics added in the mid-18th century.
The building currently houses a subsidiary of the Sanborns shopping chain.

The white population of La Palma, in northern El Salvador, specializes in the production of religious and naïf artwork
(inspired by the creations of Fernando Llort), now seen as a symbol of the country throughout the world.

Hispanic towns and great estates

If we exclude the cities such as Guatemala City, San Salvador, Managua or Panama City, rebuilt to the North-American model, the towns of Latin America are arranged according to the colonial pattern known as 'territorial', where the various communities live in groups decided by ethnic, cultural and economic criteria. These towns have three unfailing characteristics; they are horizontal, they are homogeneous and they are grid-planned. The first thing which strikes the European visitor is the regular criss-cross layout of the streets, a city-planning feature which, in the days of the colonization, was a logical result of theoretic-

ally unlimited space. The utopian ideal city, dreamt of by the Iberian architects, was seeded in this huge new greenhouse and all the great cities of the New World were therefore laid out on orthogonal lines. The colonial influence may be seen in the wide streets which divide the urban space into three great concentric zones. In the centre lies the old Spanish city with its colonial buildings grouped around a central square, the *zocalo*. Often imposing, to set the tone and exemplify the weight of the colonial power, they generally include the cathedral or main church, the presbytery or the quarters occupied by the religious orders, the town hall or the governor's palace and the fine buildings which once housed the ruling class and which today shelter the higher echelons of the administration. It is revealing to note that the *zocalo* has become the only urban space shared by all classes of society. Indeed, the cultural events (folk-dances and patronal celebrations) and popular markets are regularly held on this space once exclusively reserved for the nobility and the high-ranking bourgeoisie. A network of streets lead off from the *zocalo*, each making its way down to other squares and each lined with the facades of highly ornate churches, convents, old colonial houses with splendid patios, museums, private clinics... In the second concentric zone, we find the

cont. page 122

The Ascension cathedral in Hermosillo (Mexico)
stands as the principal colonial monument of the city founded by Agustin de Vidosola in 1742.

The town of Comayagua in Honduras boasts one of the crown jewels of colonial art, the cathedral built between 1685 and 1715.
Its tower contains the oldest bell on the American continent.

*Detail of the facade of Nuestra Señora de la Merced,
the finest colonial church in Antigua Guatemala (Guatemala),
a construction begun in 1548, completed 169 years later in 1717
and destroyed several times by earthquakes.*

The old city of Granada, in Nicaragua,
was built around the central square, the Parc Colon, overlooked by its majestic cathedral.

Most Mexican towns contain colonial buildings. The small county town of Malinalco has its main church,
seen here, whereas major regional capitals like Campeche feature long streets bordered with historic residences.

Still with its original surface, a street in Apaneca, the highest village in El Salvador.

The inside patio of the Governor's Palace in Hermosillo (Mexico), an edifice which now houses superb revolutionary and mythological paintings.

middle classes and the wealthier representatives of the working classes. Their brighly coloured little houses outshine one another across streets whose original cobbles are increasingly covered by tarmacadam. This is the zone of myriad little local shops, their pavement-stands loaded with fruit and vegetables, and of craft workshops where an entire population preserves its traditions. It is also the part of the city with the most hospitals. The third, much more sprawling, concentric zone is reserved for the natives, the forgotten fringe of society. This is the third-world zone with its shanty towns of oil-drum shacks roofed with corrugated iron and planks, its neglected streets and its rising crime figures. Here the different communities live in separate neighbourhoods according to their ethnic origins - poor half-castes, Indians, blacks and, over the last decade, Asians. Beyond this third zone lies a peripheral ring of reglemented rural space, occupied by private gardens, communal plots and factories.

Built in a valley at 4590 feet above sea level and surrounded by three volcanos, Agua (seen here),
Fuego and Acatenango, Antigua Guatemala, the former capital of the country, is the finest colonial city in Central America.

Independence Park, where Panama's freedom was proclaimed in 1903, is surrounded by various colonial buildings.
The most eye-catching is the dark cathedral with its sparkling twin towers.
Partial view of the colonial quarters, partly restored, which surround the San Gabriel convent in Cholula in Mexico, founded in the 16th century.

Despite the many agrarian reforms, voted but often poorly enforced or ignored, the great estates hitherto belonging only to the whites have not completely disappeared from the Mesoamerican landscape, even though they have now changed ownership as a result of various revolutionary movements. In Mexico, the *haciendas* have become cooperatives where the huge, formerly private estates are now managed in the name of the community. This democratization does not preclude, however, many of the Chihuahua ranches or Veracruz coffee plantations from having been secretly repurchased by the descendants of the former white

owners. The whole southern half of Central America is covered with great plantations owned by international corporations or some grand local families who, more or less covertly, pull the strings of their state's political economy. Thus the coffee production of Costa Rica has been, since the country's independence, in the hands of the descendants of three great Hidalgo families who, incidentally, also supply the country with many of its presidents and its top-ranking executives. In Guatemala, Honduras and El Salvador, gigantic latifundia are still owned by major North American corporations who carry great weight with the local governments. The economies of these countries are practically controlled today by the alliance of 'white capital' and the descendants of the local *Gachupins* or Europeans.

The Mexican city of Pueblo offers visitors an outstandingly photogenic panorama of streets bordered with great bourgeois mansions, their facades covered with local talavera tiles and their doors richly carved.

*Taxco, a very ancient mining town specializing in silverworking,
is one of Mexico's colonial jewels.*

The Indians formerly said that their lands were born of the Rainbow's rays.
Present-day inhabitants have obviously kept this innate taste for colours, as may be seen in these details taken respectively in the streets of Mexico,
El Salvador, Guatemala, Costa Rica and Honduras.

Mexican colonial houses are generally whitewashed,
a practice which allows the many decorations and ornamentations on the facade to be picked out in bright colours.

The white population
still own most of the big holdings,
whether stock parks in northern Mexico,
ranches in Honduras or latifundios
in Costa Rica.

With their rich woodwork and their dark-coloured furniture, the interiors of these colonial houses are often much more sober. Leon (Nicaragua).
Another example of Creole craftsmanship, the famous carretas, as here in Sarchi (Costa Rica).
These little multi-coloured carts were, until not more than ten years ago, the main means of transport in this mountain region.

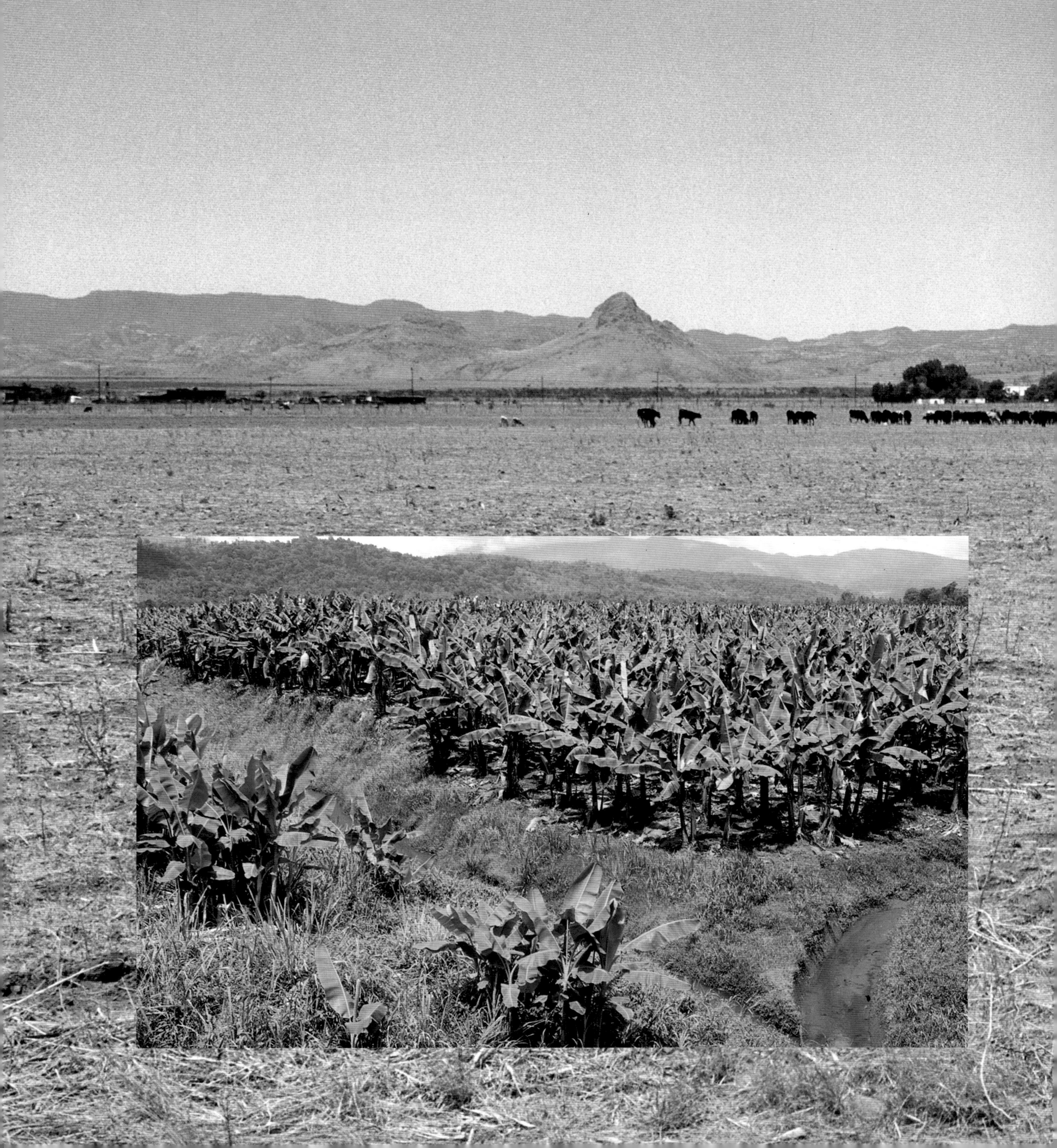

House in the highlands of Belize with the steeply sloping thatch roof characteristic of this rain-swept region.

The hair-trigger sensitivity of the mestizos

With the notable exception of Costa Rica,
the métis make up the overwhelming majority
of the Central American population.
Their very number and its economic and
political weight now enable them to take their
revenge on history, the revenge of a people,
caught between two worlds,
who were long dominated and despised by the whites
and who, they themselves, showed little leniency
towards the Indians and the blacks.

A population torn between two societies

The appearance of the *mestizos* was historically inevitable, caused by the fact, touched on above, that female immigration from Europe was very low throughout the entire period of the colonization. For other reasons perhaps but certainly through necessity, the conquerors of the New World intermarried with the Indians and, very rarely, the blacks, to ensure their own descent. The demographic progression of the 'half-breeds' was rapid and exponential. In the late 16th century, they represented less than 0.03% of the Mesoamerican population. By 1800, they had crept up to 2.4% By 1900, they represented one person in five and today they account for 55% on average of the population. These *mestizos* themselves form a sort of hierarchy according to the colour of their skins and to the social ranking often attached to it. Thus we find a scale which includes, from top to bottom, the strict half-caste (offspring of an Indian and a white person), the mulatto (first-generation offspring of a black person and a white) and the zambo (offspring of an Indian and a black person).

Culturally and socially, the *mestizos* have been victims of History. In the eyes of the first Spaniards, they were inferior, from an ethnic point of view, to the Indians whom the white colonists considered as pure-blooded. Thus initially they were rejected to the very bottom of the social scale. When afterwards, shiploads of black slaves arrived to work on the plantations and in the mines, their stock went up a little. In a society which had imported an even lower category, they were no longer considered as the bottom rung in the ladder. They then proved themselves very harsh, even cruel, taskmasters for these selfsame black populations over whom the white masters now allowed them to wield a certain authority. In the course of the 16th century, the whites began to mark a little distance with the Indians, who had accepted to give up neither their culture nor, especially, their religion, relegating them to a much less exalted rôle. The *mestizos* decided to throw in their lot with the whites, thinking that they would supplant the Indians in the social scale, a decision they were to regret, for the Indian blood flowing in their veins prevented them from entering into the European or Creole families. Their 'we-want' attitude was not at all to the liking of the whites, who ostracised them even further. As may be read in the words of Solorzano Pereira, they were harshly judged, "We see that most of them prove to be vicious and depraved and that they are responsible for most of the wrongs and humiliations suffered by the Indians". This ostracism reached the point where the *mestizos* were forbidden to train for the priesthood whereas, for at least a century, the Indians were allowed to become ministers of religion. They therefore harboured a double resentment, on the one hand against the whites, towards whom they suffered from a real inferiority complex, and, on the other hand, the Indians whom they considered as savages utterly unworthy of the privileges they were awarded. It should be remembered that Indians, converted to Christianity, had been appointed governors of the Indian republics from 1522 onwards and even *encomenderos* by the Spanish authorities from 1550. Yet the demographic catastrophe which destroyed the Indian populations was to work in favour of the *mestizos*. From the beginning of the 17th century, the whites, who had lost practically all their Indian contacts, were obliged to do business with an ever-increasing half-caste population. The latter played a particularly important rôle in the great Central American uprisings of the 19th and 20th centuries, where it formed the backbone of the revolutionary battalions led by the Creoles and where some of their charismatic leaders, such as Benito Juarez or Emiliano Zapata, became the emblematic symbols of popular aspirations.

Henceforth, nothing could be done without them and nothing was done without them - except, perhaps, in those many cases where they were manipulated and (ab)used by the authorities in power. The mestizo constituent in today's Central America may be a force to be contended with, but has the position of the 'half-breed' been clarified for all that? The answer must be no, for all the original social cleavages, founded on differences in skin colour and blood purity (differences which have still not been eradicated today), have been aggravated by financial inequalities. And the question remains for the *mestizos*; where is their place between the supposedly inferior world of the blacks, Indians and poorer half-castes and the supposedly superior world of the whites and the wealthy assimilates?

The future is theirs

Of the 128 million people living in Central America today, more than 72 million are of mixed blood. They number 5,700,000 in Honduras (an overwhelming 90% of the population), 5,340,000 in El Salvador (89%), 3,105,000 in Nicaragua (71%), 1,960,000 in Panama (70%), 51,800,000 in Mexico (55%), 4,700,000 in Guatemala (42%), 75,500 in Belize (34%) and 200,000 in Costa Rica (only 8%). Even if only because of the

The mestizos control most medium-scale farming. This three-horse team is typical of the Marcala region in Honduras whereas the little holding against the backdrop of the volcanos is Guatemalan, located near Cuatro Caminos.

These two mestizos from Santiago in Panama are just back from work on the estate of an important land-owner. They will farm their own lands in the afternoon.

landslide demographic potential they symbolize, they are the future of the subcontinent. The Mesoamerican countries were all born of the fusion of cultures and ethnic groups, a mix symbolized in the Square of Three Cultures in Tlatelolco in Mexico, where the pre-Columbian and Spanish roots combine to create the modern mestizo identity. An inscription adds the following message, "What happened on this site was neither a victory nor a defeat, but the painful birth of the mestizo people". Their thirst for historical revenge and their wish to better their place in society have made the *mestizos* the most fervent advocates of the modern world. They were the first to wear western clothes, the first to eat in the fast-food franchises, the first to shop in the city supermarkets and the first to want to 'play by American rules'. Since the past wanted nothing to do with

them, pushing them into a secondary rôle, they have thrown in their lot with the future, believing it will bring them the recognition they feel they deserve. They form the bulk of the urban middle and working classes, living in the city because they know it represents their best chance of obtaining a qualified job. Contrary to the Indians, who tend to withdraw into themselves, and the blacks, who remain outside the system, the *mestizos* try to profit from all the opportunities offered by the state structure. Thus practically 60% of the Central American métis (as opposed to fewer than 20% of the Indians and 8% of the blacks) send their childen regularly to school. Education, careers in the army and the civil service, specializations in technology, in trade or in data processing... all are seen as roads to the same end. Those who succeed and begin to scale the social ladder keep their eyes firmly riveted on the United States and deliberately turn their backs on any reminders of the past. The middle and working classes, on the other hand, by far the largest segment of the mestizo population, entertain dual relations with the Mesoamerican and the Spanish cultures. A fresh cleavage in the society of Central America may well stem from this rift between the 'upper *mestizos*', who seek to forget their origins in the western world of the whites, and the 'lower *mestizos*' who have elected to develop an authentic Mesoamerican identity in collaboration with the most progressive Indians

A little farm in the mountains of central Guatemala.

*Three scenes from everyday life: a discussion between friends in Izamal (Mexico),
a return home from market in Valle de Angeles (Honduras) and basket weaving in Nahuizalco (El Salvador).*

The Caribbean coast of Costa Rica, between Puerto Limon and Puerto Viejo, is a succession of golden beaches where time moves with the shadows of the palms.

The children of the black slaves

Most of the blacks in Central America
are descended from the slaves imported to the
New World during the colonization period.
Some were brought directly to the continent but
most came from the islands of the Caribbean,
in the 18th and 19th centuries,
where their ancestors had been shipped
during the preceding two centuries
to labour on the great estates.

The black populations are often stereotyped as 'former slaves' or 'Uncle Toms',
misconceptions portrayed by other communities and which they themselves often cultivate.

Mesoamericans or Afro-Americans?

The blacks of Central America number some 1,700,000 individuals, irregularly distributed among the various states. In terms of population, they account for a huge 52% in Belize, but only 9% in Nicaragua, 6.5% in Panama, 3% in Costa Rica, 2.1% in Honduras, somewhere around 0.5% in Mexico and Guatemala and not more than 0.3% in El Salvador. With the obvious exception of El Salvador, all live along the Caribbean coast of the continent. The black conscripts were sent to the Caribbean islands to replace the Indian labourers unable to withstand the terrible working conditions in the mines and plantations. When the conquistadors disembarked in Cuba, Haiti, Jamaica and Dominica... they found only Indians, Karibs or Arawaks. Initially friendly contacts soon degenerated into bloody conflicts and these Indian populations, defeated and then reduced to slavery despite the orders of the Crown, were put to forced labour in the great plantations and the mines where the conditions were such that none survived long. It has been estimated that, some thirty years after the beginning of the conquest, practically all the Karibs of Cuba and the Arawaks of Haiti had disappeared. In the neighbouring islands the picture was scarcely less bleak. Thus the Spanish colonists urgently needed a fresh stock of manpower, a more resistant stock and, especially, a more docile stock. Black Africa, considered since antiquity as a natural reservoir of slaves, was again called upon to provide the ideal labourers.

Although, officially, the first consignment of black slaves was sent across the Atlantic in 1510 by the Sevillian *Casa de Contratacion* which had obtained royal permission from Ferdinand, a shipment of fifty slaves had, in fact, already been freighted to Latin America some five years before. The lucrative slave trade was soon in business, exemplified by Gomez Reynal who, in 1594, was granted the monopoly for the Spanish and Portuguese territories and who alone exported some 38,250 black slaves to the colonies in the course of nine years (a stunning average of over 350 a month!). And the Spanish were not the only nation engaged in this shameful trade; almost all the Europeans dabbled in the remunerative business, led by the French, the Germans and the English.

A law dated 1571 stated that "no negress, whether slave or free, and no mulatto woman has the right to wear gold, pearls or silk, but if a free negress or mulatto is married to a Spaniard, then she may wear earrings with pearls and a necklace, together with a dress trimmed with velvet...". Two hundred years later, the Caracas edicts officially proclaimed that all the blacks and black half-breeds "bore the shameful stain of illegitimacy... and that they were socially, morally and religiously an inferior race" . Official propaganda justified negro slavery, citing the Bible to show their inferiority and insisting on their supposedly naturally aggressive nature which characterized them as being only one step removed from wild animals. Thus we find Solorzano Pereira writing of the "custom, well founded and established, of reducing to slavery the Negroes brought from Guinea, Cape Verde and other provinces and rivers...", stating that "we do so in perfect good faith, convinced that they sell themselves of their own free will or that, following the wars they engage in, they take prisoners who are then sold to the Portuguese who bring them to us."

Black populations are to be found along almost all the Caribbean coast, notably in Belize, in the region of the Rio Dulce estuary and throughout the Cayos islets in Guatemala, along the northern coasts of Honduras, Nicaragua, Costa Rica and Panama down to the province of San Blas, where their place is taken by the Cunas Indians. The demands of these Mesoamerican blacks began to be heard, perhaps belatedly, in the second half of the 16th century, notably in Panama, where the African slaves, cleverly manipulated, it is true, by one Oxenham, a lieutenant of the English pirate Drake, rose against the Spanish. Their rebellion was drowned in blood but left its mark in every memory. Up and down the coast, in all the slave zones, their rancour and hostility towards the whites took form and grew. Towards the year 1800, Humboldt noted that "these coloured people have a quick-tempered and aggressive character and, living as they do in a state of constant irritation against the whites, it is a wonder that their resentment does not fire them more often to vengeance.".

Yet paradoxically, when the revolutionary movements shook the various lands of Central America to independence, the great majority of blacks remained passive, a position frequently attracting reproach in the days which followed. The main reason behind this non-commitment was the fact that they had no more faith in the métis to resolve their problems than they had had in the whites. Left with the feeling of being constantly relegated to the bottom of the social scale, whatever the government, they distanced themselves from the other Mesoamerican communities and turned definitively towards their coloured brothers in the Caribbean zone.

Despite the official proclamation of racial equality in all states, the black populations of Central America are still poorly represented within the various national authorities. The problem of the 'black zones' is tripartite, involving social questions, economic discrepancies and cultural relations.

The Mesoamerican blacks, historically overlooked and confined to severely under-developed regions, have decided not to co-operate with the locals. Their future relations with the other communities seem compromised, to say the least.

Ambergris Cay (Belize).
These characteristic boats are perfectly adapted for navigation among the cays scattered along over 180 miles of coral reef.

One of the wooden buildings in Bocas del Toro in Panama.
This little port, located where the Chiriqui lagoon opens into the Caribbean sea, has managed to keep its charming, old-fashioned atmosphere.

The Garifuna world

The black population of Central America may be divided into two main 'families', the so-called Africans descended from the slaves brought to the West Indies (essentially to Cuba, Haiti and Jamaica), most of whom are English-speakers, and the *Garifunas*, otherwise referred to as black Caribbeans or as *Garinagus* in Guatemala. The latter are the descendants of slaves who lived on the islands of Dominica and St Vincent before being deported by the British in 1797 to the archipelagoes off Honduras, from where they spread to the mainland and interbred with the local Indian populations. They number some 350,000 today, speaking a language which is a mixture of Arawak, Spanish, French, Swahili, Bantu and Yoruba. Their main centres of population are to be found in the Livingston region of Guatemala, the southern regions of Belize, where they form practically 15% of the local population, in the Roatan islands and from Puerto Cortes to La Ceiba in Honduras and around Puerto Cabezas in Nicaragua.

The Garifuna society follows an ancient African model and is based on a predominantly matriarchal system. The mother deals with the education of the children, for whom she alone is responsible. Similarly, her voice carries most weight in matters of politics or religion. She, again, is the family member who negotiates the market price of the fish caught by her husband or who, in a shop, deals with purchase of supplies. Music and dance constitute an important part of daily life and even in small isolated communities, weekends are celebrated with festivities in the village hall. The typically African capacity for improvised collective enjoyment has very obviously been handed down intact to these far-distant American descendants. Christian festivals and more-or-less pagan commemorations are all opportunities for fun and enjoyment. Each community celebrates the anniversary of the principal events which marked the Garifunas' exodus to the various lands of Central America; the 12th of April is a holiday, for example, in Honduras, commemorating the arrival of their first free ancestors. Similarly, 1995 was a milestone year for the Garifunas, the bicentennial of the assassination of the 'Chief of chiefs', Joseph Chatoyer, the founder of the first Caribbean republic on the island of Yuremein, as St. Vincent was then called.

Two Mesoamerican blacks, a little Honduran 'African'
and a Garifuna from Belize sporting the 'national colours' of black power in his headgear.

Garifunan music and dance rhythms pulsate with percussion-driven African, Caribbean and Brazilian tempos, combined to meet the popular demand for calypso, reggae and Afro-Brazilian styles. Using drumsticks or simply their bare palms, the musicians play in time on large drums (generally three in a traditional band), on tambourines, on turtle shells, on big hollowed-out beach shells, on boxes, on metal containers of all sorts... on anything, in fact, which resonates and can contribute to the highly syncopated rhythms. Songs and melodies accompany the music and are often taken up by the listeners, producing interactive choirs where words and chorus are tossed back and forth. When the mood becomes nostalgic and the dancers begin to move to the *punta*, the singers break into sad songs which tell of the golden age when their ancestors lived in Africa.

Many of the Garifunas are Rastafarians (from Ras Tafari, the pre-coronation name of Haile Selassie) and practise a religion which combines elements from Christian theology with other, African, additions

derived from ancient animist cults. This mystical, political and cultural movement is peculiar to the blacks from the English-speaking Caribbean islands, notably Jamaica, where it took root in the 1930s. It was created by one Marcus Garvey, a preacher who had founded the U.N.I.C.A. (an association for the preservation and development of universal negritude) back in 1914 and thus launched a movement which advocated, amongst other aims, a general return to African soil.

When Haile Selassie acceded to the Ethiopian throne in 1930, becoming the Negus or King of Kings, Garvey announced that the new sovereign was the reincarnation of God and the redeemer of the black people. The Rastafarians believe that they are the descendants of one of the lost tribes of Israel and consider themselves victims of 'Babylon', the symbol of white oppression. They thus refuse certain practices of this white world (such as contraception, marriage, some medical acts...) and affirm their membership of the African world to which, they believe, they will be called one day. In so doing, they seem to have chosen to break with the other Mesoamerican communities and to assume the consequences of this parting of the ways.

As in other towns of Central America, the black neighbourhoods of Panama's capital are insalubrious and often unsafe.

4
The Mesoamerican soul

Cloaked in the subcontinent's ancestral values, the psychological and moral identity of Central America is not easily perceived at first sight. Those born in these lands, the Indians, of course, but also most of the whites and the mestizos, feel a visceral attachment to their native soil and carry in them an innate awareness of the sacred spirit, a consciousness which sometimes leads to surprising extremes.

Painting by the revolutionary artist Hector Martinez Arteche, narrating the history of Sonora, kept in the Governor's Palace in Hermosillo (Mexico).

The mother land

Central America
features some 5 810 kilometres
of coastline along the Atlantic seaboard
and another 11,030 down the Pacific coast,
giving an impressive total
of 16,840 kilometres or over 10,000 miles.
If we look at the ratio between the area of
the land and the length of the coasts,
it seems obvious that the Mesoamerican
subcontinent should have a long
maritime tradition. Yet, curiously,
this is one of the regions of the world
least turned towards the sea.

Cakchiquels hoeing corn fields in Guatemala.

The landlubber peoples

None of the eight Central American countries has or has ever had any real maritime calling. There are, of course, several major industrial ports and many little fishing villages where inevitably, as on the archipelagos, people live only by and for the sea. The longshoremen and shipwrights of Veracruz in Mexico, of Puerto Limon in Costa Rica and of Panama City or Colon in Panama, like the skippers of the little fishing boats around the Belize keys and the Roatan Islands in Honduras or the Cunas Indians from the Comarca de San Blas in Panama, all live in close symbiosis with an ocean which feeds the local population. Yet these are exceptions rather than the rule and the immense majority (over 90%) of the Mesoamerican population lives with its back to the sea, looking inland both culturally and economically.

The pre-Columbian genetics of the natives still run strong and they have remained landsmen, whether herders on the vast desert reaches of northern Mexico, peasants on the sierras, planters or farmers on the

central plains or foresters in the southern half of the subcontinent. In the teachings of the former cultures, the ocean was a place of devils and evil forces. An enlightening example of this religious fear of the aquatic world is given in the story of Tezcatlipoca and the return of the Teules (the name given to the whites by the Indians). According to the legend told in its present form by the Toltecs but shared by many of the Mexican peoples, the civilizing god Quetzalcoatl, defeated by his rival Tezcatlipoca, the god of War and Night, set off in exile towards the East

"his tears rolling down his cheeks
his tears, drop by drop, hollowing the stones"

and arrived on the shores of the ocean. There, having promised that he would return a century later to save his sons, he (either) threw himself onto a pyre and his ashes were scattered on the waves (or else) he embarked on board a large ship which disappeared over the horizon. Throughout the long centuries preceding the arrival of the Spanish, no mention was made of any expedition which might have set out to sea in search of Quetzalcoatl. Time went by as if the sea belonged to a world which in no way concerned the Indians. When, in 1419, Cortes and his men waded ashore through the Gulf waters, they were in fact arriving by the eastern sea at the end of a year, *Ce acatl* (1 reed), which exactly completed an Amerindian century of 52 years. The natives were convinced that this was Quetzalcoatl, accompanied by his train of servants, coming back as he had promised. Their illusions were very swiftly scotched and they were forced

The fertile lowlands of Chiriqui (Panama), lying at the foot of the volcano Baru,
are one of the most productive agricultural regions in the entire country.

to face the unpalatable reality that the conquistadors were by no means gods and that they had brought death with them, a striking confirmation of the idea that water and ill-luck were linked. Identical examples can be cited in Costa Rica and in Panama, where the local populations invariably sought the shelter of their forests to protect themselves first from the maurauding Karibs from the great islands lying off the continent and then from the European soldiers from the 16th century onwards. The ancient tales of Nicaragua tell of the wrath of a cacique[1], Nicaroguan, directed against two other caciques who had sided with the Spanish, *"Tell these infamous criminals (the Spanish)… from across the traitorous waters, that I hate them and that I will exterminate them and that I too could stoop to treason and lies…"*. The present population shows an equal disinclination for salt water; a plot of land, however small, is worth infinitely much more than a boat and fishing gear. The great owners are always *land*owners, never *ship*owners as in other parts of the world, and a person's fortune is still reckoned in the acreage of his holdings.

[1] a native Indian chief

A little settlement near Rivas in Nicaragua.
The Nahuas of Mexico are the descendants of the old Aztecs. Most now scrape a living from subsistence agriculture.

In the remote valleys of Mexico's western Sierra Madre,
the Tarahumaras have managed to clear little plots of earth which they till with primitive swing ploughs.

A textbook example of milpas *created by forest clearance.*
Region of Santa Cruz del Quiché in Guatemala.

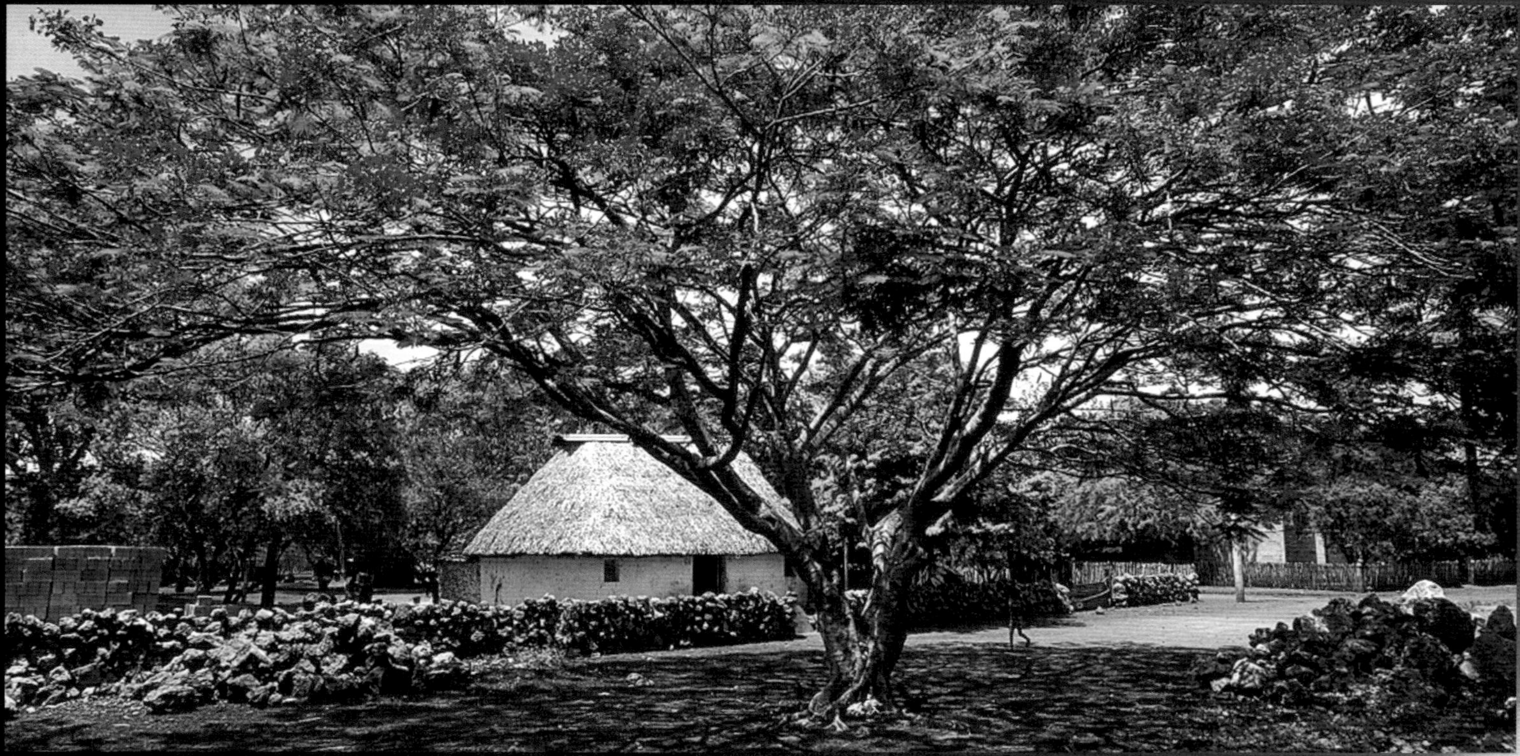

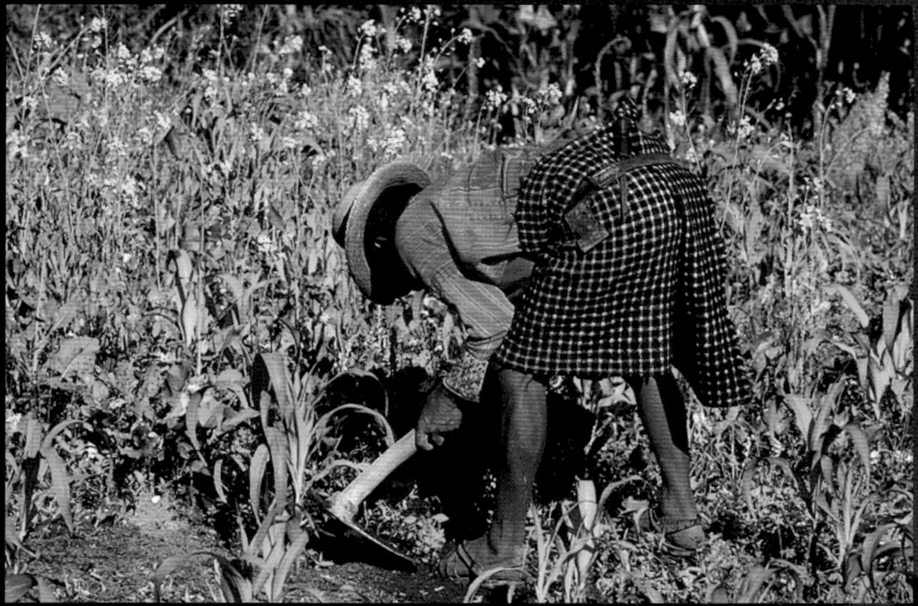

Very few of the Central American peoples are turned towards the aquatic world.
The Chocos of Panama, who always live near the lakes and rivers of the forest, are among the rare exceptions.

◁ *The Mesoamericans, and especially the mestizos, have an almost sensual love of their earth.*
The Indians carry this even further, to a degree of constant veneration.

Another 'marine' group, the Cunas who live on the Comarca de San Blas (Panama), a heavenly archipelago of islands in the Caribbean.

The Tarasques from Janitzio in Mexico are a fishing people who earn their living with 'butterfly' nets in Lake Patzcuaro.

The waters of this lake abound in pescado blanco, *a succulent little fish which is eaten fried.*

Stockbreeders in northern Mexico, Honduras and Nicaragua

Up until 1910, the economy of Mexico and all the other Central American countries depended exclusively on agriculture. From the very outset of the colonial period, huge private estates had taken shape in the north of Mexico, estates like Mayorazgo de Ibarra, where the owners held the title deeds to mines near Zacatecas and to two *haciendas* of 100,000 hectares apiece (1 000 square kilometres or 250,000 acres each), on which they raised some 200,000 head of cattle. Indeed, the very word '*hacienda*', which appeared around the mid-16th century, derives from the verb *hacer*, meaning *to make*, and thus carries the notion of some lucrative activity. Up until then, the socio-agricultural system of the New World had been based on the feudal model of the *encomienda* and the *repartimiento*, through whom the Crown or its representatives on

American soil "entrusted" and "distributed" (from the Spanish verbs *encomendar* and *repartir*) a territory and its inhabitants to a liege-lord, an *encomendero*, according to the medieval idea that the subjects should by distributed and entrusted to the good graces of the aristocrats whose task was to civilize them. Thus the haciendas, best adapted to the socio-economic conditions prevailing in the New World, continued to spread throughout the following centuries. Some covered hundreds of square kilometres. Depending on the nature of the land and on the climate, these *haciendas* specialized in quite distinct activities. In the western parts of Honduras and especially in the north of Mexico, they were devoted to stockrearing, providing grazing for vast herds of cattle and flocks of sheep. On the high tablelands of central Mexico and Guatemala, on the other hand, as in the great well-watered valleys, the *haciendas* grew cereals while those along the coastal zones added sugar-cane, coffee and tobacco to their grain harvests.

Stockrearing in Honduras is now challenged by that of neighbouring Nicaragua. Three-quarters of the production of these two countries is reserved for local or regional consumption, the remaining quarter

The Hacienda San Diego is a 1904 homestead which, until the revolution, belonged to the extremely wealthy Terrazas family, owners of a major part of the state of Chihuahua (Mexico).

being exported to the United States. In Mexico, the great northern estates work in very close collaboration with North America and their business is transacted much more across the Rio Grande than down towards the home market. The region alone produces almost 20 million head of cattle a year. The vast fattening parks of Sonora and the northern reaches of Baja California, of Nuevo Leon and Tamaulipas, all use modern feeding techniques and employ a host of veterinary specialists and qualified technicians to supply calves to the far-flung grazing grounds of Lower California, Chihuahua and various American states such as New Mexico, Texas, California, Arizona and others. The cattle are rounded up for the shows and for the various stockraising necessities (branding, vaccinations...) and the finest earmarked for the traditional events like the American rodeos or the Mexican charros. Over the last two decades, the renowned northern ranches have had to contend with competition from those of Veracruz and Tabasco who also have the North American market in their sights, notably since the signing of the North American Free Trade Agreement, an important tripartite trade treaty contracted between the United States, Canada and Mexico.

Round-up in a corral in Sebaco (Nicaragua) for vaccinations.

Another round-up, this time in the Chihuahua (Mexico), to separate the cattle already branded from those which have to be identified.
'Welcome to Maniaticos' says this signpost outside the Honduran village where a mini-rodeo is scheduled.

The horse is the only means of transport
in the great empty reaches of Baja California.

As in the past, corn remains the staple crop on small farms,
whether in the lowlands of El Salvador or the high tablelands of central Mexico.

◁ *Against a backdrop of Mexican charro: a cowboy from Sonora (Mexico) winding his lasso,*
a saddler from Nicaragua and these proud horsemen from Mexico in their elegant finery.

The small farmers from the midlands and southern regions

Every second inhabitant of Central America lives in the country and earns his living from the land. Despite falling numbers caused by the lure of the big cities over the past three decades, the peasant population remains considerable in percentage terms; 60% in El Salvador, 58% in Guatemala, 57% in Honduras, 55% in Belize, 51% in Costa Rica, 45% in Panama and 36% in Mexico and Nicaragua. In the

world of the peasants, the basic agricultural unit is the *milpa* (a Nahuatl term meaning a section of land cleared to make it arable). On these plots cleared by burning, the peasant farmer still grows, as in the pre-Columbian days, the 'American trilogy' of squash-corn-beans which forms the basis of his everyday diet.

The main result of the revolutionary movements in the 19th and early 20th centuries was that the land was returned, at least theoretically, to the people through a series of agrarian reforms. In Mexico, for example, the constitution of 1917 stated that the nation was sole owner of the agricultural land and the subsoil. Most of the great hacienda owners were expropriated and their estates transformed into *ejidos*, inalienable community lands, the local council being entrusted with the task of redistributing the various plots according to collective and individual requirements. This generous reform ran into difficulty with local 'arrangements' whereby major landowners were allowed to bypass the new law. The peasants who had not received any land continued to work for others, former *haciendaderos* or the new owners of small holdings.

A milpa *cut into the hillside*
in the Jinotega region of Nicaragua.

Despite these difficulties, the Mexican agrarian reforms have succeeded in restoring land to some 2,500,000 families in the course of three phases spread over the period from 1924 to 1982.

The agricultural situation in other countries is different. In Belize, for example, it depends heavily on overseas aid, notably from the United States, Great Britain and Canada. In Guatemala, yet another reform was announced in 1996 when the government and the guerilla freedom-fighters finally sat down and signed peace agreements. Yet pending the enforcement of these reforms, 70% of the arable land is still in the hands of less than 3% of the population and the private *latifundios* continue to prosper, notably along the Pacific coast. In El Salvador, despite the loss of its military backing, the old land-owning oligarchy has kept enough influence to block all the various agrarian reforms. The gross national products of Honduras and Nicaragua, on the other hand, rank (with Haiti) among the three lowest in Latin America. Despite

land reforms and official flag-waving, their economies, notably agricultural, are, in reality, determined by US overseas aid policy. Both these countries were ravaged by the 1998 hurricane Mitch, a natural catastrophe which annihilated most of their efforts in this field by destroying much of their agricultural potential. Aid flowed in from the international community, notably from the United States and Europe, but the future seems black for the poorer peasant farmers. Costa Rica and Panama are special cases. Nicknamed the 'Switzerland of Central America', the former has based its economy on coffee-growing since the mid-19th century. In this land with its uncommonly high white population, the great landowners and the multinationals hold the economic power. Panama, considered principally as a financial market, draws most of its resources from the canal, the banking business, the Colon free zone and from maritime trade.

If we look at Mesoamerican agriculture as a whole, three conclusions stand out. Firstly, that today's production, although varied, is simply a continuation of the colonial tradition where sugar-cane, bananas, coffee and tobacco are grown on the great estates and corn, rice, sorghum, manioc, sweet potatoes and vegetables are grown on the smallholdings and community lands. Secondly, that agrarian reforms have been introduced very unequally. And thirdly, that the lands given back to the people are often very hard to farm, either situated in the marshlands (Gulf of Mexico, floodplains of Belize, Honduras and Panama) or else in the largely inaccessible mountains (highlands of Guatemala and Nicaragua).

This Costa Rican youngster has just harvested the fruit from a pejevalle, *one of the species of palm trees that abound along the Caribbean coast.*
The main market in Managua (Nicaragua), where the peasants come daily to sell their magnificent red pitayas.

In the Gracias region of Honduras, this packman goes from village to village supplying the needs of the locals.
Pounding beans on the island of Omotepe in Nicaragua.
These haricots, together with squash and corn, constitute one of the main ingredients in the local diet.
In country regions, all good tortillas are cooked in traditional ovens.

In the fertile region of Chinautla in Guatemala, a peasant from San Juan del Sur with his solid-wheeled cart
and a high village in the Tenancingo district of Mexico. ▷

In the 16th century, after having taken Izamal (Mexico) from the Maya, the conquistadores destroyed the Indian temple of Popolchac and used the stones to build the convent of San Antonio de Padua, the largest in the Americas.

The sense of the sacred

As far back as human records go,
Central America has always been a land of religion.
The pre-Columbian cults became mixed with
European Christianity, giving birth to a most unusual
syncretic religion which, today,
without any particular embarrassment,
pays homage to the former gods and the
one-and-only god, worships the forces of nature
and still manages to respect the Christian dogma.
The sacred is an integral part of the earth -
for Christians, the earth symbolises the Creation
(Adam was fashioned from clay), the matter from
which we all are made and to which we all return.

The famous Maximon, protector of Santiago Atitlan in Guatemala, is guarded round-the-clock by the members of the Cofradia de Santa Cruz.
Easter celebrations for the Mayos in Los Mochis (Mexico).
The Indian councillors, led by the covanagua or local governor, dip the figures of their village saints to baptise them.

*Pagan-Christian offerings from a Quiché in Santo Tomas,
the main church in Chichicastenango (Guatemala).*

The many faces of religions syncretism

For the pre-Columbian peoples, everything was god, from the stars in the sky to the little happenings of everyday life. For the Aztecs, the rain was a divinity called Tlaloc. Similarly, it was deified as Cocijo for the Zapotecs, Tajin for the Totonacs and Chac for the Maya. Sifting through the mythologies, we find Yum Kax, the Aztec god of corn, and his Mayan counterpart, the goddess Centeocihuatl, who took her place in the pantheon beside Chantico, the mistress of volcanoes, Metztli, the lady of the moon, and Tonatiuh, the sun god and protector of warriors. Each concrete reality threw its own sacred shadow.

When the Spanish arrived in Central America, the struggle between men was mirrored by a battle between their gods. In Chilam Balam's book of books, a poem explains that the *"Dzules (whites) had come to castrate the sun"* and, in his history, the Spanish monk Sahagun points out that, before Tenochtitlan finally fell, the Aztec people were in tears because they knew that *"their emperor, Montezuma II, was going to submit the great gods to the Teules* (whites)". In fact, rather than simply defeated on the battlefield, the Mesoamerican people were morally and religiously vanquished by the conquistadors. Their many divinities had neither been able to withstand the all-powerful single god of the invaders and nor had they been capable of protecting their children from the terrifying weapons of their enemies whom many Indians took initially for divine beings. Yet neither the battles lost nor the dark days of the colonisation could diminish the Amerindians' inherent sense of the sacred; they simply changed their ways of worshipping the godhead. Indeed, the most

extraordinary proof of their unshakeable attachment to their culture was the fact that they never abandoned their gods, no matter how weak they had proved, but simply 'adapted' them to the new system. The impact of militant Christianity played a leading rôle in the (more or less covert) preservation of the ancestral cults. Had the determination of the conquistadors and the colonists to convert ever more souls been less relentless and had the fanatic proselytism of many of the churchmen and captains allowed the Indian soul more of a chance to breathe, then the Indian religion of today would certainly have been different. The heavier the weight of the Christian religion, the stronger the spiritual resistance of the Indians. While Central America was being covered with religious monuments - with churches, cathedrals, convents and monasteries, all architectural treasures today - the former pagan faith simply went to ground and survived in various forms hidden behind the Christian liturgy. Many examples of this remarkable syncretism still give us pause for thought. The 15th of August, the day of the Assumption of the Virgin Mary, allows many ethnic groups to celebrate the Earth Mother. The Christian festivals of Easter, Ascension Day,

Two holy places of worship in Chichicastenango: the Santo Tomas church, whose walls have been freshly whitewashed for the festivities
but which the locals, by superstition, categorically refuse to clean, and Pascual Abaj, an altar dedicated to the God of the Universe.

On holy days in Santiago Atitlan (Guatemala), the statues of the main local divinities are paraded through the town.
After the ceremony, each goes back to its respective 'house'.

Pentecost and Corpus Christi, all in honour of the life of Jesus, are also opportunities to honour the gods of the Sun, of the Corn, of the Rain... The Catholic saints often unwittingly carry an alter ego in the form of an Indian divinity who even speaks through their host's effigy (as, for example, the famous Maximon of the Tzutuhils from Santiago Atitlan, the stronghold of Indian resistance in Guatemala). When sowing their *milpas*, those small fields they clear from the forest and cultivate for a few seasons, many Indians still hail the sun, offering him some small gifts, and whistle to call up the winds. They then set a small brazier filled with burning incense in the middle of the field, kneeling to invoke the protection of the pagan gods and

the Christian god for their future crops. In other districts, at harvest time, they scatter seeds of maize to all four corners of the horizon to appease the spirits and remain in their good graces. What is perhaps even more astonishing is the fact that the local priests turn a blind eye to these practices, despite official recommendations from their hierarchy. The Church has been trying to stamp out these former cults for the past five centuries and, despite her many efforts and her frequent lapses into brutality, she has not succeeded. Making the best of a bad conversion, she has had to accept that her local representatives come to terms with the local particularities they encounter. In Chichicastenango in Guatemala and in San Juan Chamula in Mexico, today's Mayas celebrate an astonishing cult inside their churches where they pray both for their former gods and for the Christian god. The Mexical Huichols go and 'hunt' the sacred peyot (hallucinatory mescal cactus) after having been blessed by the village priest. Various carnivals, celebrating the five days of transition between the Amerindian calendars and the rising of the new sun (the triumph of the forces of Light over those of Darkness and Evil), are interspersed with masses...

There is also another syncretism, little spoken of, which concerns the black populations. The former

One of the last pictures of the old Chan Kin or Tsankin burning nopal in the kurs or sacred Mayan bowls.
This patriarchal founder of the Lacandon clan in Naja (Mexico), he was said to be well over 100 years old.

animist cults from Africa and their "American offspring", the Haitian voodoo and the Brazilian macumba, both arrived in Central America with the first shipments of slaves or refugees. The Church has firmly condemned these rites by treating them as devil worship, but yet again she has had to accept several tacit local arrangements and admit that Catholicism, to survive in these regions, had to ally herself with pagan rites cloaked in mystery and held in fearful respect by the other communities.

Creole architecture

The hyperbolic faith of the Spanish could only produce monuments on a similar scale.
The Christian faith has given Central America some of the world's finest religious edifices, exemplified in the great Mexican cathedrals built between the 16th and 19th centuries in Guadalajara, in Chihuahua, in

Mexico City (completed only in 1813), in Cuernavaca and in Puebla (the cathedral considered the best proportioned in the country), and those constructed in Guatemala City, in Tegucigalpa in Honduras, in Granada and Leon (the largest in Central America) in Nicaragua and the San Felipe cathedral in the old Panama City - all built to the European model.

The main, single-nave church is flanked by a presbytery and a monastery, completed by various typically Creole annexes, like the atrium with its huge doors and different sorts of outside chapels. There are also thousands of other churches, smaller, lower, less famous but just as beautiful. The Creole Christian religious architecture reached its zenith during Renaissance and Baroque periods, born respectively in the late 15th and 16th centuries in Italy, from where it spread throughout Europe and notably Spain, a land which heartily subscribed to the Renaissance values in the 16th century and joyfully embraced the Baroque excesses of the 17th and 18th centuries. The Renaissance brought a coherent system of architecture, with its plans, orders and modular lines, and a decoration which broke with the Gothic grotesques, foliation, medallions and pilasters, whereas the Baroque chose to astonish and to move the spectator by appealing to his senses rather than his reason, and by playing on the effects of movement and contrasts between light and shade, loading and overloading its buildings with *trompe l'oeil* effects and overabundant decoration.

In Latin America, these two schools absorbed local characteristics such as the taste for colours, for decorative elements taken from nature or the spiritual exaltation peculiar to the Amerindians. Thus Central America became heir to a colonial patrimony of an extreme richness, where many styles combine and fuse. In the 16th century, the first buildings were constructed in the Mujédar style, so-called because of the

17th century polychrome wooden statue
kept in the San Francisco convent in Grenada (Nicaragua).

name given to the Moslems who remained in Castile after the Christian reconquest of the region. The Capilla Real of the former convent of San Gabriel in Cholula, built in 1540, is a fine example with its 49 cupolas. This Moorish style can still be seen in some great houses, such as that belonging to Don Fernando Carvajal Estrada in Campeche, despite the fact that most have been replaced by other constructions considered more 'European'. Creole Renaissance architecture is magnificently illustrated by the Plateresque style, a term derived from the Spanish for silversmith, describing a highly ornamented style reminiscent of the elaborate decoration of silver plate, applied to the church facades.

The Churriguesque style, characteristic of the Spanish baroque, takes its name from three architects from Madrid, the Churriguera brothers, who created magnificent works which included carved reredos with

cont. page 182

El Salvador possesses some of the oldest small churches on the subcontinent.
Here we see the rich woodwork inside the chapel in Panchimalco and the facade of another in Apaneca.

The cathedral in Leon (Nicaragua) with the Lions fountain,
symbol of the city, in front of it.
Begun in 1747, this magnificent cathedral took a century to build
and remains the largest in Central America.

cabled columns and ornate decorative effects. This profusion of decorative elements, this obsessive attention to detail, this deliberate wealth, this use of unusual materials, all remind us of the rococo architectural movement in France and southern Germany. This style was brought to Central America by artists and architects, the most famous of whom was Lorenzo Rodriguez, who, in the 18th century, began the sumptuous decoration of Iberian facades. The Churriguresque style was enriched with typically Mesoamerican elements (decoration enriched by a sometimes excessive accumulation of detail, by a taste for the convoluted and by a mixture of pagan and Christian elements) and, after various local adaptations, gave Creole architecture some of its most magnificent expressions, notably a whole series of Mexican

The Spanish in Baja California call their churches misiones.
Here we see that of San Francisco Javier de Vigge-Biaundo, founded in 1699, which attracts pilgrims from all over on its saint's day,
every 3rd of December, and the interior of San Ignacio de Kadakaaman, built in 1728.

masterpieces like the churches of San Felipe Neri and Santa Domingo in Oaxaca, with their splendid interiors decorated with polychrome and gilded stuccowork, the church of Santa Prisca in Taxco, that of Tercera Orden de San Francisco in Cuernavaca, the Sagrario Metropolitano in Madrid, the extraordinary Jesuit church of San Francisco Javier in Tepotzotlan, which owes its splendour to transformations carried out in the 18th century (notably the stunning little Camarin del Virgen) and other superb creations such as the Golden Altar of the church San José in Panama, the Comayagua cathedral and the altar of the Tegucigalpa cathedral (celebrated for the remarkable gold and silver chasing) in Honduras, the Merced church in Granada and those of the Recoleccion and of Calvary in Leon in Nicaragua and many others.

The multi-coloured facade of the church of San Andres Xecul in Guatemala, decorated with naive figures of cherubs, unidentified fruit and the lions of the crown of Spain.

The majestic cathedral of Santiago, built in 1542 and reconstructed on several occasions after being destroyed by earthquakes, dominates the eastern side of the central park in Antigua Guatemala (Guatemala).

One of the finest bell-towers in the churrigueresque or Spanish baroque style: Santa Prisca, built between 1748 and 1758 in Taxco, Mexico.
The ceiling of the Camarin del Virgen in the church of San Francisco Javier in Tepotzotlan (Mexico).
This chapel is considered the crowning glory of the churrigueresque style.

The gold and silver baroque altar in Tegucigalpa cathedral (Honduras), built between 1765 and 1782.

The church of San José, in Panama's old town, houses the famous Golden Altar. Covered with mud by the priests,
it was the only church treasure saved when the English pirate Morgan pillaged the city in 1671.

*The same Mexican inspiration runs through this modern painting decorating a house in Metepec
and (opposite) in this ancient Mayan low-relief of a ritual decapitation in Chichen Itza.*

Death seen as a celebration

To the native fascination for blood we must add four centuries of the almost-morbid Spanish attraction for anything connected with death and the nobility of blood shed in a noble cause. Closely associated with the 'honour of the race', blood has been a constant component of the Iberian soul since the Middle Ages (a sacrificial value for the homeland or family, outstanding feats of arms, the myth of the lone knight), a permanent challenge to life. In the Amerindian philosophy, on the other hand, sacrifice was considered as a sort of soaring towards the gods, the victim being seen as a messenger from the menfolk down on earth. A sacrificial death was viewed as an honour which reflected on all the family and the clan, considerably increasing their standing in society, and was thus an occasion for great festivities.

The Spanish soldiers and pioneers first fought against the Indian peoples before interbreeding with them. The Catholic church destroyed the pagan gods but the ancient cults survived in disguised forms, intermingling with Christianity. When the characters of the two civilizations came into conflict, the weaker disappeared. But when they took markedly different paths, they grew stronger and sank deeper into the

Every Sunday the corrida attracts thousands of aficionados to the monumental Plaza de Mexico, the largest bullring in the world.

soul of the people. The conception of death is a telling example of this divergency.

To play for one's life is a "moral sport" in Latin America. Besides the corrida, imported from Spain and adapted to local tastes, certain pre-Columbian rites still survive. It is a curious fact that the colonial religious authorities never prohibited them, notably those of the Totonac *voladores* and the Quebrada *clavadistas*. Although, alas, they are mostly reduced today to a folklore spectacle for tourists in search of thrills, these two rites have come down to us from the mists of time and were originally practised in honour of the sun. The ceremony of the *voladores* has been best preserved by the Veracruz Totonacs. Five men, after a few ritual dance steps, climb a pole some ninety feet high. One of them, sitting balanced on a small piece of wood fixed to the top of the pole, begins to play on a five-tone flute and a tambourine. When the

reedy notes of the flute stop, the other four, each attached only by his feet to a rope coiled round the top of the pole, throw themselves into the air, head first and arms outstretched, and descend in ever-widening circles towards the ground. This ceremony, linked to fertility rites, is particularly symbolic in that each *volador* is supposed to trace thirteen circles round the pole, thus giving, for all four men, a total of fifty-two, the sacred figure which corresponds both to the number of weeks in a solar year and the number of years in the ritual pre-Columbian century.

The famous Quebrada *clavadistas* in Acapulco, on the Pacific coast, dice with death since 1934, the date when they restarted a very ancient fertility cult. After long prayers to the Virgin Mary... and to the local Indian gods, the divers plunge off a dizzying 45-metre cliff. Their dive must be perfectly synchronized with the wave movements below; they throw themselves out into space when the ocean has drawn back, exposing the sand and rocks of the seabed, calculating that they must reach the bottom of their dive just as a new wave comes churning down between the rock walls to catch them in its arms. The slightest mis-calculation means certain death.

The syncretic character of the Mesoamerican religion is clearly illustrated in the celebration of pagan-

Coloured skeletons and 'laughers' often ornament the facades of Mexican houses,
as here in Taxco and Guanajuato.

cum-Christian festivals. The 2nd of November is, as elsewhere, the day of the dead, All Souls' Day. Yet people take it as an opportunity to decorate their homes with multicoloured streamers and deposit flowers and various offerings (a handful of corn seed, a glass of alcohol, an amulet…) before little domestic altars. In many regions, the children are given presents of little, brightly coloured, sugar skulls and the spectacle of them delightedly crunching these grinning craniums amid popular rejoicing, with music, dancing and singing, but also amid prayers and lamentations for the dead, is a sight quite surreal to European eyes. In

Mexico City, great humorous skeletons are burned to 'unite the living and the dead in laughter'. In the Maya region, the bodies are exhumed and carried to the family home, where they are laid under the table to share in the family meal, before being taken back to the cemetery. During the major village festivals, coloured skeletons, grimacing demons or slack-jawed skulls are hung on the facades of the houses or from the ceiling of the main room. In general terms, the link between the worlds of the living and of the dead remains unbroken. Unlike Europeans and North Americans, the peoples of Central America remain in permanent contact with their dead, consulting them on a whole range of subjects, going to speak to them in the cemetery or dining with them on their tombstones. Do they fear death less than we do? Has life less value in their eyes than the store we place in it? A certain fatalism and a sense of natural continuity between life and death, between generations past and to come, certainly enables them to shrink less from their fate, to allay the fears which beset us. Where we see the dread reaper, they see an inevitable associate.

Mexico has preserved two of the most astonishing pre-Columbian rituals in Central America,
the clavadistas *in* La Quebrada *and the* voladores *in* Papantla.

Detail of one of the monumental revolutionary friezes which decorate the walls of the Governor's Palace in Hermisillo (Mexico).

Revolutions, revolutions!

The history of Central America
is punctuated with innumerable revolutions,
immortalised on walls painted by recognized artists,
like the Mexicans Diego Rivera
and Clemente Orozco, and the anonymous
muralists whose works adorn the urban landscapes
of Guatemala and Nicaragua.
This violent land has always declared its
fierce desire for independence,
but has never been able to win that liberty
without copious bloodshed.

The Creole rebellion of the 19th century

No matter how ferociously they were repressed or how determinedly the missionaries tried to convert them, the Amerindian peoples never accepted the Spanish domination.

The 17th and 18th centuries were officially calm but in fact abounded with small yet recurrent rebellions, both Indian and Spanish, and it was not until the 19th century that the nations of Central America finally gained their independence. Society had evolved during the intervening years. Massacred, deported and humiliated, the Indians no longer formed the majority of the population. They had been replaced by the rising tide of *mestizos* whose gunpowder sensitivity made them potential revolutionaries. They needed leaders and the Creole community supplied them. To understand the history of the later revolutions, we must ask ourselves why these Creoles allied themselves with the Indians, the *mestizos* and the blacks against the European power. Their main motivation was the bitter rivalry which separated them from the *Gachupins*, that social élite composed of European-born Spaniards who held all the political, religious and military powers. Their haughty pride, their absolute refusal to cede or share one iota of their prerogatives and their visible disdain for these American-born 'false Spaniards' so exasperated the Creoles that the latter decided to play a purely American hand right to the end, whatever the stakes, and they thus became the ideological instigators and often the military leaders of the revolutionary movements.

The Mexicans blazed the trail, taking advantage of Joseph Bonaparte's territorial claims on Spain's American possessions. When Napoleon I named his elder brother King of Spain and the Indies, the rebels proclaimed their fidelity to Ferdinand VII, the legitimate sovereign, and the long-awaited clash between the Creoles and the Spaniards became inevitable. In October 1810, spurred on by the priest Miguel Hidalgo, 80,000 men stormed the towns of Zacatecas, San Luis Potosi and Valladolid before defeating the loyalist armies at the battle of Las Cruces, near Mexico City. Yet they did not dare attack the capital and this was their downfall. They went on to take Guadalajara but were shortly afterwards defeated by their adversaries who had had time to muster their forces. Hidalgo, betrayed and taken prisoner, was executed together with several revolutionary chieftains in 1811. Another priest, José Maria Morelos, took up the combat and set siege to Mexico City. He convened a congress of representatives in Chilpancingo and several measures were adopted, including abolition of slavery, suppression of royal privileges, universal suffrage and the sovereignty of the people. Morelos was, in turn, captured and executed in 1815. His army, dispersed, transformed itself into bands of guerrilla fighters who proved terribly effective (notably the group led by Vincente Guerrero in the state of Oaxaca), harrying the loyalist troops and offering little opportunity for counter-attack. By 1821, the military pressure on the country was such that the viceroy, Agustin de Iturbide, accepted to make terms with Guerrero before finally breaking with the Spanish Crown and having himself proclaimed Emperor of Mexico. The situation of the country remained confused until 1823, when Iturbide was deposed by General Antonio Lopez de Santa Anna, who proclaimed the republic of Veracruz in December 1822. The following year, the new president had a constitution voted, based on the American model, which established the federal republic.

In that same year of 1822, five other lands of Central America - Guatemala (which then included Belize), Honduras, El Salvador, Nicaragua and Costa Rica - set up a federation called the United Provinces of the Centre of America. This fragile union, supported, as in Mexico, by the Creole élite, brought to power men as different as the conservative General Arce and the liberal Morazan. Contested by the local chieftains, it collapsed seventeen years later, in 1839, undermined by the rising forces of nationalism.

The Mexican epic of Juarez, Villa and Zapata

While Mexico was marching to the military tune of Santa Anna, Honduras was changing its constitution according to the military or civil governments which succeeded one another and El Salvador was grappling with a long Indian uprising, led by Anastasio Aquino, before suffering a long series of coups d'état. This state of affairs was suddenly interrupted by the astonishing 'Walker episode'. William Walker was an American filibuster who, in 1853, at the age of 29, invaded Baja California with a troop of mercenaries and set up the Republic of Lower California and Sonora, of which he proclaimed himself president. Pursued by both American and Mexican troops, he fled two years later, with 56 men, to Nicaragua where the liberals of Leon had called him to support their struggle with the conservatives of Granada. After carrying off a series of victories, Walker had himself appointed president of Nicaragua! The USA recognized his government with a rapidity which prompts suspicions that the entire 'Walker episode' was a puppet operation organized by Washington to consolidate its grip on Central America. Walker first repealed the anti-slavery laws and then made English the official language before launching his celebrated slogan, *'five or none'*, by which he claimed the presidency of the other regional states. In 1857, he was defeated by a

coalition of these same states and, to avoid being taken prisoner, surrendered to the American navy. After two unsuccesful attempts to re-establish himself in Central America, he finally returned to Honduras where, unfortunately for him, he was captured by the British, handed over to the Honduran government and executed in 1860 at the ripe old age of 36.

In the meantime, Central America was mired in particularly troubled circumstances which verged on anarchy. Mexico, above all others, was in particular difficulties. In 1845, the United States decided to annex the once-Mexican territory of Texas, which had declared itself independent through pressure from the American pioneers. War broke out between the two countries. The Mexicans of Santa Anna were defeated and American troops invaded Mexico shortly afterwards. To the south, the Mayan Indians, armed by the British settlers in Belize, took the opportunity to secede. In a movement known as the 'Caste War', they rose in 1847 against the great landowners who had despoiled them for centuries past. In the north, the Mexican government signed the Guadalupe Hidalgo treaty with the US in 1848, ceding an immense

These photos from the early years of the 20th century show two of the emblematic figures of the Mexican revolution,
Emiliano Zapata on his horse and Francisco Pancho ('Fatty') Villa with his wife.

territory made up of Texas, California, Utah, Colorado and most of New Mexico to the United States. Five years later, with the 1853 Gadsden agreement, the Santa Anna government sold the rest of New Mexico and Arizona to its American neighbour. The Mexican people, already stung by the humiliating defeat, were not to put up with this new infamy and Santa Anna was overthrown by the Ayutla revolution of 1855. Benito Juarez, a Zapotec Indian, became the new leader of the government. The subsequent promulgation of several laws (sale of Church possessions, redistribution of land to the people...) triggered the

Reform War between the Vera Cruz liberals and the conservatives of Mexico City. When liberals won the day and Juarez became president, the French, with the agreement of the English and Spanish, decided to send an expeditionary force to support Maximilian von Habsburg, chosen as Emperor of Mexico by Napoleon III. The new master of Mexico, soon abandoned by France under pressure from the United States, was defeated, captured and executed three years later, in 1867. Juarez again became head of state, remaining president until his death in 1872, whereupon a liberal named Porfirio Diaz swept to power at the head of a new uprising. During his presidency, which was to last 33 years, Mexico went through a period of relative stability. The country developed and peace reigned on the home front, except in the Yucatan, where soldiers cruelly punished the Maya to such an extent that, by 1901, half the local population had perished. Throughout the rest of the country, the peasants were gradually dispossessed of their lands and saw them given over to the great estate owners. Strikes and demonstrations were put down by the army

A colossal statue, 120 feet high,
stands on the highest peak of the little island of Janitzio (Mexico) in honour of José Maria Morelos.

and, in 1910, the great Mexican revolution broke out, led by charismatic chiefs who galvanised followers from all the lower and middle classes without any distinction of race. These leaders were Francisco Madero, Francisco 'Pancho' Villa and Emiliano Zapata. Diaz resigned in 1911 but Madero the moderate could not curb the demands of the more radical leaders such as Zapata and thus the country slid, once again, into civil war. After proclaiming the Ayala plan to give all the land back to the peasants, Zapata and his troops defied the regular army. Local chieftains throughout the land took control over their own territories and

the country went through a period of total anarchy. In 1913, after the 'tragic ten days' which had witnessed the start of the bloody counter-revolution, General Victoriano Huerta deposed Madero and became the new president. Backed by the United States, he only succeeded in exasperating the people even further. A fresh revolution broke out, led by Pancho Villa, Venustiano Carranza, Alvaro Obregon and Emiliano Zapata. Soundly defeated, Huerta relinquished his grip on power but the victors were unable to agree and began to fight amongst one another, Villa and Zapata against Carranza and Obregon! The latter pair proved the stronger and Carranza, named president, declared a new constitution in 1917. Zapata alone carried on the struggle, but Carranza had him assassinated in 1919. The following year, he himself was executed by his former ally, Obregon, who in turn proclaimed himself president. When Pancho Villa was assassinated in 1923, the last of the great revolutionaries was removed from the board of a bloody power game, ending a civil war which had claimed almost 2 million victims, mostly from among the civilian population.

Detail of one of Diego Rivera's revolutionary paintings from the walls of the National Palace in Mexico.
His companion, Frida Kahlo, is represented here helping the disinherited.
'The Revolutionaries', one of the frescoes painted by Clemente Orozco in the former Jesuit college of San Ildefonso de Mexico, now a museum.

The nationalist uprisings in Guatemala, El Salvador and Nicaragua

When we look at how the protest and then rebellious movements began in Central America in the 19th and 20th centuries, we notice that they were all linked to the American appropriation of an economy bequeathed by the Spanish. Through the intermediary of its soldiers and pioneers, the Spanish Crown had imposed a European-style political order and an extensive mode of agriculture controlled by the great estate owners. By the early 19th century, each country had become specialized; El Salvador produced coffee and indigo, Costa Rica furnished coffee, Honduras was the banana state and Guatemala grew bananas and coffee. Work on the plantations was almost always carried out by the *mestizos* and blacks, the Indian population having been largely decimated in the 16th and 17th centuries. Working conditions were dreadful and the standard of living extremely low. In the aftermath of independence, all these countries fell prey to American interests. Standard Fruit (originally Vaccaro Bros.), Cuyamel Fruit, United Fruit and other huge corporations established veritable agricultural empires served by obedient local governments. Life degenerated to such an extent for the Mesoamerican peoples that popular uprisings broke out almost everywhere - only to be crushed by ruthless action from the army and private militia. Soon the USA no longer troubled to hide its activities, intervening directly whenever the interests of the great corporations were threatened. In 1932, during a peasant and Indian uprising led by the El Salvadoran Augustin Farabundo Marti, American military advisors assisted the El Salvadoran army who massacred over 30,000 people in the course of the infamous *matanza*. In 1954, disquieted by the rise of communism in Guatemala, the USA orchestrated an invasion of the country from Honduras. The Guatemalan president, Jacobo Arbenz Guzman, the man who had instigated a sweeping agrarian reform and nationalised several of the United Fruit properties, was deposed, his agrarian reform nipped in the bud and United Fruit given back its holdings.

Agriculture went through an unprecedented boom in the 1960s and 70s yet the richer the great corporations and the governing oligarchies made themselves, the poorer the people became. Uprisings, at first episodic, began to spread and multiply.

In Guatemala and El Salvador, the revolutionary movements organized themselves as guerrilla forces and both countries sank into civil war. Although communist officers and aides from the USSR and Cuba helped in the field, these uprisings had a genuinely nationalist undercurrent. The main movements were the Marti National Liberation Front in El Salvador, and the Guatemala National Revolutionary Unit. The dictators in place showed few scruples and the main targets were the Indians or 'those who appeared Indian', killed out of hand in the name of the struggle against communism. In the beginning of the 1980s, faced with the extent of the massacres and worldwide reprobation, the USA gradually ceased to support the local dictators but imposed a sort of blockade on countries considered hostile. Throughout the rest of this decade, Guatemala and El Salvador lived a smouldering war punctuated by regularly broken ceasefires. Peace agreements were finally signed in 1992 in El Salvador and four years later in Guatemala. The statistics of these wars make terrible reading: 200,000 tortured and killed in Guatemala, over 10,000 unaccounted for and a million left homeless; in El Salvador, 75,000 slain and almost a million forced to emigrate to neighbouring lands or to the USA.

Nicaragua, which had briefly belonged to Mexico, gained its independence from Spain in 1821 before becoming part of the Confederation of United Provinces. Beginning in the mid-19th century, it lived through a political situation unique in Central America. Although relatively untroubled by problems with its neighbours, it was torn by the bitter rivalry between its two main historic towns, Leon in the north, poor and liberal, and Granada in the south, rich and conservative. At around this same period, the English and the Americans were considering digging a canal to link the Pacific with the Caribbean, a project which was to take best advantage of Lake Nicaragua. Matters were interrupted by the Walker episode, and when this filibuster had made his exit from the Nicaraguan political scene, his allies, the liberals from Leon, fell from power and were replaced by the Granadan conservatives who, to the further chagrin of their rivals, transferred the seat of government from Leon to Managua in 1857. In 1893, a nationalist general of liberal views, José Santos Zelaya, came to power. The United States, already jaundiced by the defeat of the conservatives, stirred up troubles which firstly forced Zelaya to resign and then prompted the people to rebel. Seizing these uprisings as a pretext, the American marines disembarked in Nicaragua in 1912, imposing American peace terms until 1926 and reinstating the conservatives. This conservative government was challenged in 1928 by increasingly active liberal groups with, at their head, men such as José Maria Moncada, Bautista Sacasa and Angusto Sandino, the self-styled "general of free men". The Americans left the scene, leaving behind them the Nicaraguan National Guard they had trained. General Anastasio Somoza, head of this Guard, first had Sandino assassinated, and then Sacasa, before having himself elected president in 1937. He himself was later slain but his sons took over and continued his policies, creating a reign of terror, pillaging the country shamefully, eliminating their opponents and amassing a colossal fortune. Driven to extremes, the people rose in protest several times under revolutionary banners such as Carlos Fonseca Amador's Sandinist National Liberation Front and Pedro Chamorro's Democratic Liberation Union. Fonseca was assassinated in 1976, Chamorro shared his fate two years later and each of these movements was beaten down by the National Guard. The Sandinists finally overthrew the last

Somoza in 1979. The United States, who had supported the dictator, allowed him to seek asylum in Paraguay where he was finally discovered and slain by a Sandinist commando unit two years later.

Nicaragua was in ruins. The Sandinists and their allies, moderates and Marxists, squabbled over which path to follow. During the presidency of Jimmy Carter, the United States initially accepted to help the new power to rebuild the country but policy soon took a radical turn under the influence of Daniel Ortega Saavedra and military advisors, engineers and technicians flowed in from the Soviet bloc and from Cuba. When Ronald Reagan came to power in 1981, American policy changed abruptly. After cutting off all aid to Nicaragua, the new president supplied an anti-Sandinist rebellion composed of mercenaries and former National Guardsmen, known as the Contras. The Sandinists and the Contras engaged in a terrible struggle which was to last until 1990. Over 100,000 men were involved, losses were tremendous and many civilians died in what were then termed 'dirty conditions'. Although condemned by the International Court of Justice, the USA continued to bankroll the Contras with funds from sales of arms to Iran, sales prohibited by the UNO embargo. The American press revealed the scandal, the famous Irangate, and Washington was obliged to abandon its allies. The Sandinist National Liberation Front held a monopoly on all state powers and cut itself off from its popular support base. In 1990 and then in 1996, Ortega and the Sandinists lost the general elections, ceding their place to a centre-right government created from the Liberal Alliance signed between the partisans of the Chamorro clan and supporters of the Aleman faction.

Two paintings from the town of Jinotega, characteristic of revolutionary art in Nicaragua. The first decorates the interior of the Central Sandinista and the other covers the outside walls of the former prison where the dictator Somoza was incarcerated.

5
Tales of masks, pottery and weaving

The rising tide of the modern world gradually erodes, day after day, the bases of traditional society. The arts of mask-making, pottery and weaving, so ancient and yet so enduringly popular, remain one of the fields which have best resisted.

◁ *Magnificent stag's head created by the Mexican Huichols using tiny multi-coloured beads fixed to a wooden frame.*

The art of the mask and the dance

Formerly used for ritual ceremonies,
for theatrical performances
and as a propitiatory ornament for temples,
the mask is now most associated
with all the popular celebrations
in Central America,
the folklore events and
the religious festivals.

Easter celebrations for the Quiché people in Guatemala.

The ancient tradition of the mask

The mask played a fundamental rôle in all the pre-Columbian civilizations. As might be expected, since the most important symbolic figure in Central America was that of man himself, anthropomorphic masks have been discovered almost everywhere. We know that actors and dancers wore masks, like the Greeks and Romans of antiquity, during sacred theatrical performances and for secular festivals.

Stelæ and low-reliefs show priests and shamans using what were often other types of masks. The priests chose divine characters, to help them enter into magic communication with the gods, while the shamans, seeking to participate in the mysteries of the supernatural world, opted for representations of the good and evil forces of nature.

The mask was also closely bound up in the funerary ritual. Various series of archæological excavations have brought to light superb burial masks decorated with semi-precious stones, some made of wood, others of stone, ceramics or, more rarely in pre-Columbian times, of gold. The most famous have been unearthed in Teotihuacan, in the Mixtec region, and in the Mayan lands, notably at Palenque in the Chiapas (where the superb mask of King Pakal was discovered), at Calakmul in the eastern reaches of the Yucatan, at Tikal and in other sites. Carved by artists in relation to some higher reality, the mask was supposed to transmit its magic powers to the wearer but was also seen as an idealised image of the deceased. This psychological approach, similar to that of the ancient Egyptians, meant that the wearer identified himself with his own lineage and with the long line of his ancestors. Rich materials were employed because their value had to be comparable with their noble mission. Thus we find the Teotihuacan pieces decorated with mosaics of onyx, serpentine, pyrite, jade, jadeite and turquoise, incrusted with mother-of-pearl, obsidian or shell, while those of the Maya are made from pieces of jade, often decorated with turquoise, obsidian and mother-of-pearl. Other types of half-funerary half-magic masks have also been discovered in Central America, made from stone in the Olmec areas, from jade in Talamanca in Costa Rica or from wood, like those of the Nicaraguan Chorotegas.

As the propitiatory face of a divinity, the mask, in its wider sense, was employed unceasingly in ancient architecture. The faces of the gods stare at us everywhere, carved and moulded on household objects or decorating the walls of grand monuments. The Mixtec gold pectoral plates from Monte Alban, with their delicate ornamentation of spirals and flowers, and the Aztec vases and finery were all decorated with representations of the main gods such as Mictlantecuhtli, Xipe Totec, Coatlicue or Xochipilli. The heads of Tlaloc and Quetzalcoatl look down from the sides of the Quetzalcoatl temple in Teotihucan just as those of the Mayan Chac glower from the buildings in the Yucatan, the most famous example being the Cod Poop or 'Wall of Masks' in Kabah, ornamented with 300 effigies of the rain god. Indeed, the Mayas, more than others, made frequent use of these gigantic masks, aligning them along the bases of temples and palaces and using them to frame wide flights of stairs in the aim of impressing the spirits even further and underscoring the sacred character of the site. Famous examples include those at Edzna, Xpujil, Coba, Kohunlich, Tikal and Xunantunich. From the Gulf of Veracruz to that of Chiriqui, the local custom was to use the supposed powers of the mask for magic purposes, to communicate with the supernatural, to contact the dead, to call up the powers of the earth or the skies or to change one's personality.

There were two types of masks, the sacred ones referred to above, and the secular versions. It would seem that the ancient peoples of Central America made the same use of these latter masks as we do today. Everyone must have noted how, during a masked ball or a carnival, people enjoy pretending to be someone else and how disguises often throw a very different light on various personalities. We also know that when a person's face is hidden, he allows himself to behave in ways he would not normally, a little as if the 'protection' of the mask allowed him to give rein to his basic impulses by freeing him from moral and social taboos. The popular masses of Central America, long fettered by European shackles, use the mask in conjunction with dance as an opportunity to settle their accounts with the colonisation they suffered.

Detail of one of the walls at Codz Poop de Kah in Mexico.
The facade of this Mayan 'palace' is covered with some 300 masks of Chac, the rain god.

*This ritual mask, worn by the Mayos from Sinaloa in Mexico during religious ceremonies,
is supposed to represent the forces of evil which assail the saints.*

Indian dances, a revenge on the past

The Amerindian peoples dance whenever they can, for births and weddings, for funerals and anniversaries of deaths, before sowing and harvesting, when the rains begin, during the summer and winter solstices, for Christian festivals and for Independence Day... Imprinted in their soul, dance steps constitute a triple affirmation of their Indian identity: their continuation of ancestral tradition, their resistance to European order and their revenge on history.

Associated with secular theatrical performances and religious ceremonies, dance occupied an important

place in the various Mesoamerican cultures before the arrival of the Europeans. Of the many survivals which have come down to us, the stage epic of Rabinal Achi, over 3 000 verses long, is one of the few to have been preserved intact. This dramatic Mayan ballet shows us, in a series of arresting tableaux, the capture of a Quiché prince by the warrior Rabinal, his judgement and his sentence to death in the court of King Hobtoh, 5-Rain. Side by side with this highly elaborate aristocratic form of ballet, we also find various types of popular dance with a largely symbolic content. Thus the Emberas from Darien in Panama tattoo or paint their faces during the festivities leading up to the New Year or during various 'magic moments' in the lunar or solar years. In northern Mexico, the Mayos and the Yaquis still practise the 'buck dance' in honour of their sacred totem animal. These two ethnic groups live in relatively self-sufficient societies containing several religious congregations which, according to an ancient rite, the members join after making a vow. Each congregation must supply its quota of dancers to perform during the great pagan-cum-Christian festivals. Closely linked to hunting and agrarian rites, the dance involves one or two performers wearing bucks' heads, representing the forces of Good, with, opposite them, a group of masked

cont. page 208

Already performed long before the Spanish conquest,
the Buck Dance is of primary importance for the Mexican Yaquis.

dancers (often coyotes) who symbolize the spirits of Evil. The 'struggle' may last several hours, the dancers moving to the sound of dried gourds, filled with pebbles, tied to their legs, and to the chants of the spectators. After all sorts of incidents, the coyotes, killed by the buck, are transformed into men armed with bows and arrows... who finish by shooting the noble animal. The famous *voladores*, mentioned above and still found in many regions of the subcontinent, are another remarkable survival from the pre-Columbian past.

Besides these purely Amerindian ritual performances, there are other, highly popular, dances which result from a mixing of European and Indian currents. When the Spaniards arrived, they brought with them other models which the locals gradually adopted, adapting them to their own taste. In the early days, the Indians were content to accept this new repertoire, such as the 'dance of the Moors and Christians' or the 'dance of the Moorish king', which illustrated the tale of how the Spanish kings expelled the Arab invaders from their territory. But very soon they began to add new characters, Indians of course, who introduced themselves into the story, sometimes as allies of the Spaniards, sometimes as 'wise men' that the Spanish came to consult. As one of the only modes of expression left to the native dancers, this new content gradually took on ironic overtones. Defeated on the battlefield, decimated by illnesses, deported and sentenced to hard labour, forcibly converted by the missionaries, the Indians were condemned to mask their feelings and to take a covert revenge in mockery. And here, starting in the late 16th century, the Indian mind came into its own, showing an inventive genius and a scathing humour rarely equalled on the stage. The Phurépéchas of Michoacan skewer their oppressors in the 'dance of the little old men', a performance rife with their barely veiled contempt for the Spanish aristocracy and administration. The 'little old men', wearing wrinkled face masks with cheeks and lips outrageously farded, coiffed with ridiculous over-white wigs and cramped in foolishly narrow clothes, totter and limp about the stage, tripping and sometimes falling, to the glee of the assembled spectators, all delighted to poke fun at European society. At Paabanc, near Coban in Guatemala, the traditional July celebrations are an opportunity for identical performances which, behind other masks, make fools of the conquistadors, the Spanish settlers and all their descendants. Yet it is in the dances relating the conquest itself that the real pain of the Indians is best seen. The 'Conquest dance' of the Guatemalan Quichés, the 'dance of the Great Conquest' of the Nahuas and the 'feather dance' of the Mexican Zapotecs all tell the same story: the arrival of the conquerors and their struggle against the Indian chieftains. Alvarado against Tecum Uman in the first, Cortes against Montezuma in the other two, they all follow the same chronology, outlining first the initial encounters between the future adversaries, continuing with the theme of premonitory dreams (the Indian leader seeing the destruction of his people in his sleep), and ending with the defeat and heroic death of the chieftain. The actual endings do differ, however, allowing us interesting insights into the Indian perception of this watershed in their history. While the Nahua myth insists on the heroic death of Montezuma, crystallising him in legend as the implacable enemy of the Spanish, the Quiché dance presents a surprising scene of reconciliation and fraternization between Mayas and Spaniards over the body of the fallen hero, Tecum Uman. More surprising still is the end of the feather dance, where history is reversed and Montezuma imagined as the victor! Taken prisoner, Cortes tries to commit suicide in his prison but is prevented by the Aztec emperor, who pardons and frees him. Overwhelmed by such generosity, Cortes swears that he will never again harm the Indians! This type of happy ending is found in other religions as, for example, in that of the Sonoran Opatas (who claim descent from the ancient Aztecs) where the 'Degüinemaca dance' ends with the signing of an eternal peace treaty between those brothers in combat, the Spaniards and the Indians. These multiple variations were certainly a form of balm for the Indian soul, a means of masking a reality which wounded them and a psychological opportunity to digest the injustices they had suffered and soothe their resentment.

The masks created by the craftsmen from Chichicastenango in Guatemala are the most highly renowned in all Central America.
The character of Pedro de Alvarado plays one of the two main roles (the other is the Mayan chief, Tecum Uman)
in the Dance of the Conquest performed by the Quichés in Guatemala.
The Phurepechas from Jaracuaro used their satirical Dance of the Little Old Men to ridicule the colonists and European nobles.

*All the versions of the Dance of the Conquest and the Great Conquest feature two opposing groups of dancers/actors
who mime the bloody clashes between the Indians and the Spanish in the 16th century.*

In the Tzeltan culture in Amantenango del Valle in Mexico, the pottery is always made by the womenfolk.

The age-old tradition of the potters

Pottery is one
of the oldest human productions
and remains one of the keys to help us
understand the daily life of long-gone peoples.
Today's Central American potters have simply added
their own artistic sensitivity
to an exceptional heritage of pre-Columbian
traditions they continue to perpetuate.

Two splendid examples of masetas,
the great storage jars made by the Pokomams in Chinautla (Guatemala).

Physical and magical contact with the clay

Archæological excavations have furnished us with tens of thousands of pottery artefacts, secular and religious, whose types and decoration form a sort of pattern book, allowing us to turn its pages and discover the tastes of the ancient peoples, their diet and the ways of cooking, their everyday clothes and the burial costumes, their religious rites and their daily habits, their crops and their craftwork... All these objects indicate that the physical contact with clay, that universal material from which all life springs and to which it all returns, has always been a part of the Mesoamerican traditions. The Olmecs were perfect masters of both the coil-pot technique and the art of moulding. Their brown three-legged urns and vases, strictly cylindrical or flaring slightly towards the top with incised patterns picked out in red, were

decorated with coloured slips and engraved with ritual motifs. The city-state of Teotihuacan produced a good deal of painted pottery, often decorated with sea-shells. Cooking-pots with or without handles, bowls and plates with moulded rims, braziers, three-legged vases in the effigy of gods, candle-holders and crockery have all been found in quantities. Many are in one single colour, the commonest shades being red, ochre, black or coffee-coloured. The Zapotecs and the Mixtecs have left us funerary urns which are veritable terracotta sculptures (representing the great gods of the Waters and of the Lightning, the Bat god, the Sacred Glyph god and others), together with zoomorphic and anthropomorphic statuettes whose hands and feet often finish in jaguar claws. The designs are geometric and repetitive, painted in colours of fawn, black, red, blue and brown.

The most impressive legacy of pottery has come down to us from the ancient Mayas. They created all sorts of objects (household and sacred utensils, three- and four-footed funerary vases, statuettes...), characterized by their refinement and elegance and skilfully decorated with polychrome slips on which human and animal figures and hieroglyphic signs were painted or incised. The Aztecs were famed for the extreme precision of their pieces and the delicacy of their decoration. Generally burnt-orange in colour, their pottery was decorated firstly with geometric patterns and then later with figurative representations of

The potters' district in Solola (Guatemala) attracts many visitors on market day.
The famous 'black vases' of San Bartolo Coyotepec are the pride of Oaxaca state in Mexico.

animals and flowers in very vivid and varied hues. The Toltec potters developed their own characteristic style with simple yet elegant forms and understated decorations, typically off-white in colour and incised with rows of fine wavy lines. The Totonacs, on the other hand, produced a highly glazed, bright red pottery against which their polychrome motifs stood out boldly. The Chorotegas and the Nicaraos preferred contrasts too, decorating their creations with strange half-human, half-animal figures painted with red and black-brown pigments. The Veraguas culture in Panama had a penchant for large dishes decorated with intricate and convoluted drawings of birds, dragons and mythological serpents. Their neighbours, the

Tonosi, went even further, creating even more tortured designs in dominant shades of black and brown where the staring, distracted eyes ringed with concentric circles in the middle of stylised, almost giddy faces remind us curiously of African art. As we can see, styles varied enormously and those described above are simply examples among many others.

A woman from El Porvenir in Honduras turning receptacles.

One very special feature of Mesoamerican pottery is the fact that the contact between artists and craftsmen has remained unbroken down through the generations. Today's potters perpetuate ancient traditions and have even, in the course of the past century, reinstated typically pre-Columbian subjects, such as representations of the old gods, long banned during the colonisation. The potter's clay is a symbol of this continuing life cycle. The potter himself, who shapes it and gives it life, is considered as a sort of magician, making tangible the invisible. In former times, he held a special position in society and was greatly respected by his fellow citizens. Today, even though social and psychological conditions have changed greatly, potters are still highly thought of and still surrounded by an aura of mystery; they know secrets of creation hidden to common mortals. A historical study of Mesoamerican pottery allows us to draw several conclusions. Firstly, that this art has always been ritually linked to the very site of its production; the form and decoration of pieces hew very

closely to the specific 'cultural profile' of each given people. Secondly, that the choice of colours corresponds to the way rites and mythologies have adapted to the presence of materials chosen by Nature to represent any given group. Each Mesoamerican zone had its own colour: ochre in northern Mexico, the land of sand, red in the central regions where the peasants till the rich red loam, green in the Mayan lands, carpeted with their lush forests, black in Nicaragua, the volcanic heart with its bubbling lava... And lastly, that the sacred and the secular are never really separated, that many everyday objects are employed in rituals and that religious symbols (stars, and latterly crosses) are often used to decorate household utensils.

The craftworkers from the El Valle region of Panama specialize in large elegant jars and stylized animals.

An exceptional diversity of styles

Today's Mesoamerican pottery has kept that dual character, both sacred and secular, of its ancient fore-bears. Potters' workshops are found throughout the subcontinent, turning out both ordinary household ware and much more elaborate decorative pieces. During the colonial period, these craftsmen were all Indians, but today, although certain very specific productions are still Amerindian, many *mestizos* and whites have also entered the field.

The reputation of certain centres of production has spread well beyond their region and attracts buyers and visitors from afar. The most reputed are to be found in Mata Ortiz, Ihuatzio, Metepec, Puebla, Dolores Hidalgo, San Bartolo Coyotepec and Amatenango del Valle in Mexico, Chinautla and Rabinal in Guatemala, Siguatepeque in Honduras, Ilobasco in Costa Rica and in Llano Bonito in Panama.

The potters of Mata Ortiz proudly continue the tradition of the ancient Paquimés. The inhabitants of this

little village in the state of Chihuahua, formerly called Pearson, use the same local raw materials, the same techniques and the same decorative styles and patterns as the Indians did from the 10th to the 16th centuries. Painted mostly in black, white and reddish-brown, the desert animals and plants are depicted in the same stylised manner with bold and relatively rectilinear strokes. The famous 'black vases' are another local speciality. These are works of great finesse, requiring considerable skill and are particularly delicate before they have been fired. They are first covered with a black slip and then polished with a piece of quartz until a metallic sheen is achieved. Various designs are applied with a black matte paint and the pieces are then fired in underground kilns. In Ihuatzio, in the state of Michoacan, the Phurepechas, as did their distant ancestors, create splendid vases and dishes in daring forms, principally reddish-ochre and white, decorated with delicate geometric designs in black and ochre. Further south, the Metepec workshops in the state of Mexico specialize in producing great human-faced suns and moons, directly inspired from the ancient pre-Columbian cults, and especially the highly symbolic 'trees of life', also known as 'Jesse trees'. These polychrome clay constructions, highly complex, include a host of figurines made in moulds handed down from one generation to the next. They represent the synchretic universe of the Indians and the whites, assembled on branches attached to a common trunk representing the unicity of divine creation, and contain a whole series of clay figures, animals, skulls, skeletons, saints and mythological creatures. Each figurine is moulded from a combination of very fine red clay and thicker yellow clay, left to dry before *cont. page 221*

The little village of Mata Ortiz in the Mexican state of Chihuahua has continued the ancient art of the Paquimés.
Its pottery, black or decorated with traditional motifs traced with natural pigments, constitutes a direct link with the past.

One of the last craftsmen in Ihuatzio (Mexico) to carry on the Tarasque tradition,
characterized by the use of three ritual colours (black, white and ochre-red) and geometrical patterns.

*The village of Metepec in Mexico is famed for its large 'trees of life',
made in the form of chandeliers and sometimes over three feet high.*

The finest talavera workshops in Mexico are to be found in Puebla.
These well-known ceramics take their name from the Spanish town where the style originated.

being ground and mixed and then again kneaded with water to form a paste which is bound with a mucilage derived from tule flowers. After having been allowed to rest for a while, this paste is modelled and then fired before being painted. Ever since colonial times, two cities, Puebla, in the state of the same name, and Dolores Hidalgo, in that of Guanajuato, have specialized in the art of *talavera*, a very fine type of pottery which takes its name from the Spanish town near Toledo where this sort of work was originally produced. The Spanish had noticed that the same type of clay as that back in Talavera was to be found in the vicinity of these two towns. And since the two regions had already been major pottery centres in pre-Columbian times, it was easy for the Europeans to teach the new style. The bulk of today's production in concentrated on crockery and tiles, decorated with varied, brightly coloured designs which skilfully combine European and Indian influences. Many houses, notably in Puebla, boast magnificent facades in *talavera* tiles. Following tradition, this work is carried out in several stages: the modelling of the object, a first firing in a moderate kiln, the decoration, a second firing in a hot kiln and the final application of a lead and pewter glaze. San Bertolo Coyotepec, in the state of Oaxaca, is also famous for its 'black pottery'. Invented only a few decades ago, this technique consists of firing the pottery with quartz to give it a special sheen. Using two saucers as a wheel, the craftsmen mould the pots and then fire them in buried kilns. The high iron oxide content in the clay gives the finished pieces their characteristic black colour. The Tzeltal Indians from Amantenango del Valle, in the state of Chihuahua, are famous for their traditional pottery, produced using pre-Columbian methods. The various utensils and figurines are not fired in a kiln but simply set on the ground and surrounded by a ring of burning wood. The Indians feed this fire constantly and the resulting slow baking gives their work its highly characteristic patina. As we can see, Mexico hosts a wealth of pottery styles and traditions, still very much alive today.

The situation is equally healthy in the other lands of Central America. In Guatemala, for example, the Pokomam Indians from Chinautla, a little village lying just north of the capital, produce fine pottery of an ochre or brick red colour, mainly in the form of great storage jars, flowerpot holders, called *massetas*, and small vases called *tinayas*. They employ an ancient pre-Spanish technique which consists of not completely firing pottery, leaving it to partially dry by itself. The pieces are then finished, not by painting, but with little discs and other add-on decorations. In the town of Rabinal, in the lower Verapaz, the local potters have cleverly introduced modern lines (candle-holders, crockery and notably chocolate cups) into the traditional production (storage jars, funerary urns...), all made in their own original style. The region of Siguatepe in Honduras is scattered with villages where almost all the families make pottery, the best-known workshops being in El Pervenir and Esnacifor. Here again, we find a mixture of decorative, utilitarian and traditional pieces, all decorated after firing. Using extremely fine brushes, the local youngsters paint them with pagan and Christian motifs before applying a final glaze which is left to dry in the open air. One of the best known pottery centres in Costa Rica is Ilobasco, famous for its *sorpresas* ('surprises'). Found in many homes across the land, these are little round caskets (often in the form of an egg, an orange, an apple, an walnut...) which, when opened, reveal charming little scenes, called *tipicas*, drawn from daily life in the villages and fields. Over the past few years, to the great chagrin of the religious authorities, who have tried in vain to prevent them, local artists have come up with the idea of including erotic scenes (suggestive and more explicit) in their *tipicas*. More restrained, the inhabitants of the El Valle region in Panama produce figures, often life-sized, sitting sleeping sheltered from the sun under wide sombreros, painted in vivid colours. Centred in Llano Bonito, the most reputed craftsmen draw their inspiration from nature, creating a whole range of decorative objects in the form of snakes, iguanas, lizards, monkeys, cats and other creatures, all in astonishingly lifelike postures. They also continue to produce the great storage jars used down through generations since pre-Columbian times.

The sorpresas from Ilobasco in El Salvador hold charming little scenes of daily peasant life called tipicas.
◁   *A potter from Rabinal in Guatemala putting the final touches to a huge jar.*
'Sitting people' - a local speciality for the potters in Llano Bonito in Panama.

Sheltered from the rain by the roof of her home, an Indian woman from the Mams people in Guatemala weaves cloth on her belt loom.

The dazzling Indian costumes

Central America
is famous for the beauty and variety
of the cloth the Indians weave.
The descendants of the Spanish and the *mestizos*
have long since adopted western-style dress,
but many of the Indians have remained faithful
to their traditional costumes which,
although rarely worn in town,
continue to illuminate the countryside,
the mountains and the forests.

A respect for custom

The Mesoamerican arts of weaving and dyeing have remained unchanged since the late 18th century. The cloth and the clothes, so specific to each of the different Amerindian populations, are interwoven with ancient customs and European additions. Our modern world has fed industrial fibres and, especially, artificial colourings into the formerly closed loom of traditional weaving, yet despite this, most of the Indian cloth in Central America is still made according to methods which have scarcely changed in 2 000 years. The new materials and techniques imported by the Europeans from the 16th century onwards have simply helped extend the weavers' range. In pre-Hispanic times, in addition to pelts and pounded bark, the various species of agave supplied most of the raw materials. After steaming over a fire to evaporate their water content, the leaves' fibrous pulp was then carefully scraped, dried and tied in hanks ready to be spun. In the 16th century, the Spanish introduced cotton growing and sheep rearing, two imports which were to revolutionise the craft of weaving. Those living on the cold highlands preferred cosy wool while those in the hot, humid lowlands naturally opted for cotton. Today's Indians continue to prepare these two materials in the same way as their forefathers. Cotton, first cleaned of its seeds and leaves, is piled on a cloth on the ground and beaten with sticks. The shorn fleeces of the sheep are first washed, then dried in the sun before being carded with rectangular combs with metal teeth. Both can then be spun on a spindle or wheel, the latter being more rapid. As a final stage before the actual weaving, the weavers calibrate their warp according to the length of the cloth to be installed on the loom.

Most cloth is still woven on traditional roller looms which have remained unchanged since pre-Columbian times. Various systems are used but the womenfolk still prefer the belt loom. The warp threads are stretched longitudinally between rollers which divide them into two sheets. The upper roller is held by two cords tied to a tree or to a doorpost and the lower is attached to a fairly wide cloth or leather belt strapped round the weaver's hips, thereby allowing her, by shifting her position, to adjust the tension of her cloth at all times. Among the looms imported from Europe, the upright pedal version is most used for weaving long lengths. Heavier to use, this apparatus requires mainly male weavers, who generally work together in village co-operatives. With the warp threads stretched horizontally or vertically on a large rigid wooden chassis, the weaver operates his loom manually, alternately lifting the odd and the even threads by shifting frames inside the chassis, passing his weft threads to and fro with a large shuttle.

At least a score of different weaving techniques are employed. The commonest are the plain weave, the twill weave, the double weft (which gives reversible fabrics) and the marbled weave. For this last-mentioned technique, the threads are knotted in bundles and then plunged into vats of colour to produce a characteristic tie-dye effect. They are then dried, untied and woven, giving a striking speckled appearance to the finished cloth.

Despite the introduction of industrial dyes, many communities continue to make their own natural dyes from vegetable, animal or mineral pigments. The indigo-plant, for example, provides a whole range of shades from blue to violet, the Mexican cochineal gives a rich crimson and the *caracol purpura* a purple violet, different sorts of bark produce various browns and iron oxides supply yellows. Modern synthetic dyes are being increasingly used, however, because they are cheaper, easier to obtain and offer a wider and more vivid range of colours. A sad but nonetheless highly attractive example of this tendency may be seen in the little Cakchiquel village of Santa Catarina Palopo in Guatemala, where all the clothes are predominantly blue, a colour rare in the Mayan world. One day merchants came to offer monochrome blue thread at irresistible prices... the temptation was overwhelming and the old customs were soon supplanted.

A Huichol woman from Bolanos in Mexico embroidering traditional designs.

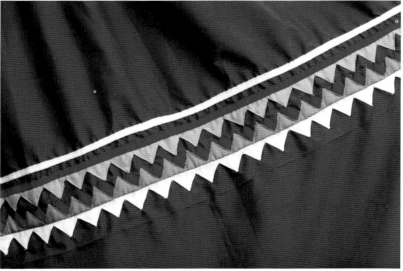

Over the past ten years, the Cakchiquels from the village of Santa Catarina Palopo in Guatemala have adopted shades of blue,
a colour otherwise very rarely used by the Maya. Traditional sketches of costumes worn by the Guaymis in Panama.
They are stylised representations of the underworld and the celestial world in their mythology.

Magic symbols of ethnic membership

Defeated by the conquistadors, decimated and enslaved by the settlers, humiliated by the Church for practically four centuries, neglected by the revolutionary movements of the 19th and 20th centuries, the Indians have nevertheless managed to conserve a considerable part of their traditional way of life in their religious ceremonies, their dialects and in their crafts. Their ethnic clothes are worn as badges of freedom and can be read, by those who recognize their language, as coded histories of the various communities.

In many regions, the traditional dress was abandoned very early, notably in the cities and in those countries where increasing western influences went hand in hand with a swooping decline in the Indian population. In the Americanized cities like Hermosillo, Monterrey, Acapulco, Guatemala City, San Salvador, San José or Panama City and in the traditionally Spanish towns such as Mexico City, Guadalaja, Tegucigalpa, Managua, Granada or Leon, it is rare to meet Indians in traditional dress in the street. Another interesting tendency is the fact that the men have shed their costumes much more than the womenfolk. Society tends to assign women the role of guardians of custom and this has certainly contributed to their staunch defence of their traditional dress. The menfolk have much greater contact with the modern world (in the course of seasonal crop-picking, shopping or job hunting) and now, under greater pressure to "dress like everybody else", tend to wear their old costumes only for ceremonial events.

Indian clothes carry a whole series of symbols, the most important of which concern fecundity and the harmony of the universe. According to ancient beliefs, found throughout Central America in various forms, human beings were created by demiurges or genii in close relation with the sun, the moon and the stars. Cut off from his stellar sources, man is doomed to decline or disappear, hence the importance of cults

A craftsman from Santa Ana in El Salvador working on an upright pedal loom.

linked to sun worship, to the mysteries of the sky and its comets, to the renewal of centuries, the appearance of natural phenomena, the conception of superposed worlds and suchlike. The cloths of lower Mixtec Indians, such as those of the Belize Mopans, are embroidered with stylized stars and, in the Chiapas, the *huipils* (sort of blouses) of certain Tzotzils are covered with diamonds, in the form of a cube and a 'four-angled hollow space', representing the earth and the sky. Other clans have figures of scorpions, animals considered to attract lightning and clouds. The monkey is seen as the harbinger of a catastrophe or the sign of some past cataclysm and thus closely associated, on cloth, with the idea of past or future creations. Anthropozoomorphic motifs represent the forces of nature found in all the Amerindian mythologies. The belts of the Huichols feature serpent symbols, identified with rain and fertility, the same role as that of the toads found on the cloth made by the Pantelho Mayas. The Panamanian Guaymis embroider their women's clothes with geometrical figures symbolising the underworld and upperworld, a theme also

seen, adapted to local taste, in the dress of the eastern Mayas and the El Salvadoran Pipils. Two-headed animals (notably eagles) are found almost everywhere, from the central Mexican Nahuas to the Cunas, for example, where they represent a dualistic vision of the world. Similarly, references to the fertility of the earth and, by correlation, to the fecundity of the womenfolk, appear in many forms on the Indians' cloth. In the Mayan zone, by far the most creative and the most prolific, various animals (peacocks, hummingbirds, cocks, vultures, bucks, jaguars and opossums) and plants (flowers, cacti, agaves and sacred trees) are associated with one another because they are thought to promote the reproduction and growth of the species. Certain insects, such as bees, dragonflies or butterflies, protect the germination of crops whereas others, like snakes and lizards, watch over the harvests.

Three types of traditional Mayan cloth, produced respectively by the Yucatecs from Mexico,
the Tzutuhils from Guatemala and the Chortis from Honduras.

A Indian woman from Comarca de San Blas (Panama) making one of the famous molas
(layered assemblies of embroidered cloth) which have made the Cunas famous.

The last male costumes

With the obvious exception of the loincloths still worn by certain forest peoples, like those in the Panamanian Darien, very few genuinely pre-Hispanic male costumes now remain. The only Indians who still dress in practically the same way as their far-distant ancestors all live in Mexico - certain Tarahumaras groups, the Tacuats and the Lacandons. The first live in the deep canyons which cut into the western ranges of the Sierra Madre in the state of Chihuahua. Their costume consists of a white loincloth (the *tagora*), a sort of plaid (the *purua*), two or three metres long, wound round the hips, and sandals (the *huaraches*) whose shape has changed little since pre-Columbian times. It is sometimes completed by a very loose, pleated shirt, in some vivid colour, and a black or white bandana knotted round their forehead. The Tacuats live in hamlets around the village of Zacatepec in the lower Mixtec. Their traditional dress is quite

astonishing, made up of a white shirt and what might be described as large white shorts, both embroidered with geometrical, stellar, zoomorphic or floral designs. The Lacandons from the Chiapas forest are the last survivors of a Mayan ethnic group who emigrated from Guatemalan Peten in the 18th century. Their costume is simple, a long tunic of rough white cotton, sometimes decorated with black or red spots produced by berry juice.

Almost all the other traditional male costumes are the result of a slow mixing of Indian and European fashions. The result is always surprising, sometimes remarkable. The most original costumes are those of the Huichols, the Tzotzils and the Tzeltals in Mexico, the Cakchiquels, the Tzutuhils, the Quichés and certain groups of the Mams in Guatemala. With the exception of the Nahuatl-speaking Huichols, all the others belong to the Mayan group. One common denominator is their footwear; all favour the same pre-Columbian sandals. The Huichols live on the ranches of the Sierras de Berberia and Nayar. Their costume is quite exceptional, consisting of a white, long-sleeved, tunic-shirt (the *rahuero*), cross-stitch embroidered with animal and geometrical motifs, and loose white trousers (the *shaversh*) decorated like the shirt along the lower legs. The *rahuero* is pulled tight at the waist by several colourful belts and, below them, a cord hung with a dozen or so embroidered purses decorated with red pompoms. A palm-fibre hat (the *roropero*) is adorned with tufts of red wool and, for those men who have taken part in the ritual 'peyotl hunt'

For the inhabitants of Todos Santos in Guatemala,
evening coffee after a long day spent working in the Cuchumatanes highlands has now become a tradition.

In the remote regions of the western Sierra Madre in Mexico,
the Tarahumaras have preserved one of the last genuine costumes from pre-Columbian America.

(a sacred hallucinogenic cactus), with birds' feathers. The Tzotzils and Tzeltals constitute the dominant ethnic groups in the Chiapas and have kept some of the most original native costumes to be found in Mexico. Their dress, which varies from one village to another, indicates both their clan membership and their social status. Thus the unmarried men generally wear a pale-coloured loose shirt, gathered at the

waist by a leather belt which also holds a wide piece of cloth tucked between the wearer's legs like a loincloth. The married men, on the other hand, wear a rough sleeveless overshirt, either in some dark, solid colour or else bright and embroidered, and knee-length or calf-length trousers. The hat has great symbolic importance and may be wide-brimmed or brimless, decorated with multi-coloured ribbons or pompoms... The *alcaldes* or town councellors have their own special costume with a generally black background decorated with a wealth of richly coloured motifs. The Mams live in the Cuchumatanes Sierra and each village, according to Guatemalan tradition, has its own traditional dress. Those from San Juan Atitan and from Todos Santos are the most famous.

In Zacatepec, in the lower Mixtec, following a custom dating from well before the Conquest,
the Tacuats still embroider their clothes with stars, flowers and stylised animals.

The menfolk from the former wear a chasuble-type tunic of thick brown cloth over a gaily coloured shirt and white trousers whereas those from the latter prefer striped shirts with long, carefully embroidered collars, and red trousers with white stripes. This gay combination is completed with black overtrousers, survivals of the pre-Columbian belt-cum-loincloth called the *maxatl*, and a stiff straw hat. Many groups of ethnic Mayas live in the highlands of Guatemala, especially in the region of Lake Atitlan. They include, notably, the Cakchiquels, the Tzutuhils and the Quichés, most of whom have remained faithful to the traditional men's costumes. Although, inside each ethnic group, there are sub-groups, clans and villages,

all with their own specific styles, certain characteristically general features do stand out. The Cakchiquels, for example, favour cowboy shirts with very stylised, colourful zoomorphic motifs. The *delantale* or *ponchito* (a brown and white checked woollen breechclout) is either worn alone (in Nahuala, for instance) or over richly embroidered trousers (in Solola). The Tzutuhils also share the taste for cowboy shirts, but in other colours and with other designs. Their trousers, white striped in black and embroidered with mythological and astral signs, stop just below the knee and are worn with a long coloured scarf wound round the waist. The Quichés now wear their traditional costume almost only for festivals and ceremonies. A magnificent sight, especially the versions worn by the *alcaldes* and the priests, it comprises a bolero jacket and large black shorts, both picked out in red and resplendent with red and blue drawings, and a bright *tzutz* or ritual scarf, knotted round the wearer's head, with long fringes hanging down to his shoulders.

The syncretism between Indian and European fashions is perfectly illustrated in the dress of these two Mayans from San Juan Atitlan in Guatemala and the magnificent costume of this Mexican Huichol woman.

The glittering costume of the womenfolk

The womenfolk's costumes are so numerous and so varied that any attempt to describe them seems practically impossible. A whole book would be needed. They represent the most complete survival from the pre-Columbian past that we have. Although the men's costumes often had to come to terms with modern society, the women's were better able to resist the various pressures and, in the event of major constraints, adapt to new economic and social factors. For today's wearer, her costume is measured according to three yardsticks; it must be in line with tradition, it must identify her as belonging to some ethnic group and it must be attractive. Each ethnic group has its own system of everyday and magical references. Inside these groups, each clan has developed its own cultural and æsthetic peculiarities. And in the clans, each family adds its own personal touch. Furthermore, to add to this multiplication, each village

strives to distinguish itself, if only by pride, from its neighbours. And, within the village, all the different social rankings must be reflected by differences in the clothing. The finest and most varied costumes are to be found in Guatemala, where the Indians form 50% of the population, and the most modest in El Salvador, a land containing less than 5% of Indians.

As was the case with the men, the Mayan lands deserve special mention for the exceptional wealth of their costumes. The traditional pre-Columbian Mayan fashion in the lowlands included a white dress decorated, along the collar and especially along the hemline, with gaily coloured embroideries of large flowers. The highland ladies dressed differently, preferring a long *huipil* (a straight, slipover garment worn as a blouse) and a skirt girdled by a wide belt. Social rankings and wealth were indicated by the quality of the cloth and the delicacy of its decoration. Today's dress has scarcely changed, the only Spanish additions being the *tzute* (a rectangular piece of cloth worn on the head or as a little cape) and the *reboso* or shawl. Without dwelling in too much detail on the decorative elements, certain characteristic colours may be mentioned. Thus, with the Cakchiquels, the women of Patzicía prefer predominantly red *huipils* while their sisters in Solona favour a mixture of bright colours and those of Santa Catarina Palopo choose shades of blue. In Santiago Atitlan, the Tzutuhils wear white or mauve short-sleeved blouses, hatched in black and em-broidered with multicoloured motifs, and a remarkable head-dress created with a ribbon of red cloth

Three traditional costumes still worn by the mountain Indian women:
a Mixtec from Mexico, a Cakchiquel from Guatemala and a Mexican Zapotec.

Like many of her compatriots,
this Huichol Mexican lady wears a blouse and long skirt combination tailored from synthetic material bought in town.

several metres long, attached at one end to a lock of hair, rolled tightly round the head and held in place with an embroidered braid. In the Quiché area, ladies' tastes seem to be for fine *huipils* decorated with ruffs from the colonial period, either in white lace (in Santa Cruz, for example) or embroidered in gay colours (as in the Totonicapan region). The inhabitants of Nebaj, on the Ixil lands, wear magnificent white *huipils* richly brocaded with multicoloured motifs in predominantly green and yellow tones, a red skirt and, to complete the effect, a superb headdress finished with large pompoms.

Away from the Mayan zone, other ethnic groups such as the Mexican Zoques and Triques, also boast some remarkable female costumes. The Trique womenfolk may be particularly noteworthy, dressed in a fine red huipil, long and loose-fitting, with horizontal stripes and fringes (which are more richly decorated for the unmarried girls) and a multicoloured *enredo*, but down in Panama, the Cuna ladies flaunt the most original outfits. In this ethnic group, the women are famous for their *molas*, living tableaux of cloth incrusted and appliquéd with animals and flowers. These *molas* are the latter-day transposition of ancient costumes forbidden by the missionaries. Completed with a short skirt of dark blue material, printed with traditional yellow motifs, wound tightly round the hips (the *saburé*), a red and yellow scarf (the *musué*), a gold nose ring and, especially, dozens of bead bracelets and anklets (*winés*), this costume remains one of the most outstanding in all Central America.

As a general rule, women's costumes are simpler and less exuberant outside the Mayan area. A long dress, resulting from mutual pre-Columbian and European influences, is standard wear. In Mexico, for the

*The traditional costumes of these two Tarahumaras from the Batopilas region of Mexico
and this Guaymi from Almirante in Panama are clearly influenced by western fashions.*

Nahuas, the Totonacs, the Mixtecs, the Zapotecs and others, it is chosen white, decorated with bright embroideries on the collar, sleeves and hemline, and set off with various colourful accessories such as a belt, bracelets and necklaces, pompoms, a headband or a scarf. The Panamanian Guaymis prefer blue, orange, pink or green versions, decorated with geometrical motifs and lines in two or three contrasting colours. In many ethnic groups, the women have simply adapted the costume worn in their village at the time of the Spanish colonisation, adding new elements to it episodically as dictated by changing circumstances. The

quechquémitl (a short tunic with an opening for the head) and a long skirt-and-bodice combination is becoming more and more popular throughout the subcontinent. Adepts include the Tarahumaras, the Tepehuans and the Coras, the El Salavdoran Pipils, the Huichols, Mayos and Yaquis in Mexico and the Lencas in Honduras.

Another widespread tendency is the halfway-house fashion of adding Indian decorations to standard European attire. Even those in the very conservative Mayan lands - the Chontals and the Chols in Mexico, the Mopans in Belize or the Chortis, the Pokomchis and the Kekchis of Guatemala - are now succumbing to this mode. Elsewhere, western-style dress has now taken over, the only difference being that the Indians, being poorer, wear cheaper and shabbier versions. Indeed, the standard garb of some of the Indians along the Caribbean coasts of Nicaragua and Honduras (the Sumos, Ramas and Miskitos), the Panamanian Chocos and the Costa Rican Borucas and Bribris is now a sorry sight when compared with the splendours that once were.

The Quiché ladies from Santa Cruz in Guatemala prefer their huipils
with wide 'Spanish-style' ruffles.

6
The Mayan example

The Maya are proud of their brilliant civilization, one of the high points of human achievement. Guardians of remarkable accumulated knowledge and of a highly advanced culture, they had lapsed into a sort of apathy, following the collapse of their great city-states, when the Spanish suddenly appeared. Despite the violence and pressure of the conquest, they have never accepted integration on European terms.

◁ *The* chac mool *from the Warriors' Temple at Chichen Itza in Mexico. In the form of semi-reclining figures, these altars (borrowed by the Yucatán Maya from the Anahuac Toltecs) were destined to receive the hearts of sacrificed victims.*

The Greece of the New World

The Maya attained a degree of civilization
unknown elsewhere in the New World.
Their knowledge of medicine,
of astronomy and of mathematics,
the refinement of their art,
the inventiveness of their architecture
and the originality of their literature
have won them the sobriquet of
'Greeks of the New World'.

The great pyramid at Labna (Mexico), topped by a temple nicknamed El Mirador.

The ancient Mayan script

The Maya are the only people of the American continent to have invented a system of writing which is sufficiently extensive and precise to allow all forms of thought to be recorded in a combination of codified signs. From the late preClassic period onwards, they began to transcribe their texts on long rolls of bark paper coated with lime (the codices), on the stelæ and on the carved stones. During the Classic period and, to a lesser extent, during the post-Classic era, Mayan literature developed to a spectacular degree and its output was still considerable when the conquistadors dropped anchor. In the name of Christianity, so many

Two magnificent stelæ. The one covered with hieroglyphs was discovered at Tikal in Guatemala and the other,
featuring a feathered dignitary, at Xunantunich in Belize.
Reproduction stela erected in situ at Tikal, depicting a ritual ceremony.

masterpieces were destroyed - works beyond price today - that only four have come down to us! The bishop Diego de Landa burned thousands of scrolls in the infamous auto-da-fé he lit in the Yucatan in 1562. Yet it was through this iconoclast, quite involontarily and as if by some ironic twist of destiny, that the Mayan writing was first deciphered. He had carefully studied the culture he was so determined to destroy and, characteristically, noted the hieroglyphic signs in his *Relacion de Las Cosas del Yucatan*, notably those relating to the calendar, thinking that they were merely a straightforward alphabet. Thus he recorded the names of the days and of the months and their corresponding glyphs. In the late 19th century, the international community began to take great interest in the vanished civilizations of Mesopotamia, Egypt, Persia, India... and the Mayan lands. Information was compiled and documentary sources explored. The actual deciphering of the Mayan language was begun by the abbé Brasseur de Bourbourg who, in 1864 and quite by chance, stumbled on Diego de Landa's work. The French priest noticed that the signs reproduced

were also to be found in the Madrid codex and on various inscriptions carved on monuments in the Yucatan, the Chiapas and Peten, analysed the parallels and paved the way to a partial deciphering.
Almost all the ancient words were monosyllabic. They were represented by phonetic glyphs which were sometimes so stylised that the object or concept represented was difficult to recognize. Each glyph was made up of a main sign-root onto which other secondary signs were grafted (prefixes, suffixes, prepositions, determiners...). Depending on their position on the glyph, these could modify the meaning of the root and almost a dozen combinations of these different elements were possible for one single root. To complicate things further, the artist, whether painter or sculptor, could modify the glyph for purely æsthetic reasons, omitting secondary signs which were repetetive or adding others which had no bearing on the meaning but were simply visually attractive! Hence the extreme complexity of a system which has still not been completely fathomed. Furthermore, since glyphs only represented concrete objects, abstract notions could only be conveyed through concrete glyphs - an additional source of confusion and errors. Glyphs could be replaced by 'associated signs' and the same glyph can thus possess three different values, a process which greatly complicates our reading of them. Although all the Mayan manuscripts have now been deciphered, most of the inscriptions engraved on the monuments, made up of different glyphs, still keep their secret.

The Quirigua site in Guatemala features some of
the highest stelæ in the Mayan world.

The invention of the calendar and of zero

Although history credits the Maya with the invention of the Mesoamerican calendar, this is not quite the case. They did indeed perfect the calendar, bringing it to a hitherto unequalled degree of perfection, but rather than creating it themselves, they improved a model left them by the Olmecs. Archæological excavations in the Olmec zone have brought to light various calendar glyphs linked to a system of bars and points which represented figures. Probably invented towards the year 800 BC, this prototype Olmec

calendar defined a year of 260 days divided into periods very similar to the future *baktums, katuns, tuns, uinals and kins* of the Maya.

The Mayan priests, fascinated by the regular return of the seasons and by the constant passage of the stars, very soon concluded that our world was regulated by fixed natural laws. Acting on this premise, that the universe was a cyclical process, they went on to reason that careful study of the past should allow us to better understand the present and, especially, to foretell the future. This philosophical and metaphysical approach was the foundation stone for Mayan science and one of its first creations was the famous calendar or, perhaps should we say, calendars.

Indeed, drawing on generations of daily observations made by the priest-scientists, a highly complex set of complementary systems was devised to measure the passage of time. The two basic systems were the *tzolkin*, a ritual year of 260 days, made up of 13 months each lasting 20 days, and the *haab*, a civil and solar year of

Partial view of the Copan main square in Honduras with its famous stelæ carved almost in the round.
Stela C can be seen in the foreground.

365 days, composed of 18 months of 20 days and an additional group of 5 unlucky days called the *uayeb*. The different units of time were the *kin* (day), the *uinal* (a month of 20 *kins*), the *tun* (a year of 18 *uinals*), the *katun* (a period of 20 *tuns*) and the *baktun* (a period of 20 *katuns*). The whole set was perfected by the introduction of the 584-day Venusian year (the duration of a synodic revolution of the planet Venus) and a new time division called the *choltun* or Long count, a grand cycle of 13 baktuns (13 x 144,000 days, giving each *choltun* a grand total of 1,872,000) which could be theoretically repeated indefinitely. A cycle of 9 nights was then defined, each belonging to a different divinity, and another of 7 days, governed by the gods of the earth. This system, extraordinarily precise, meant that no given date would be repeated before 374,440 years had elapsed.

Each of these various calendars locked perfectly with the others. With the cyclical permutation of each month, the start of the *tzolkin* and the *haab* coincided every 52 years, a period which became the Mayan century called 'the full circle of the calendar'. Similarly, two of these Mayan centuries (ie. 365 days x 104 years = 37,960 days) were equivalent to 65 Venusian years. The only remaining key to the system was the

determination of a starting date for the very first *choltun*. After protracted ritual calculations, the priests decided that this would be *4 ahau 8 cumhu*, the 13th of August 3114 BC. After all these long-term preparations, the Mayan civilization did not even survive to see the end of its first *choltun*, which comes to its close on the 23rd of December 2012...

A Mayan date thus comprised at least an 'initial series' of six signs in the following order: the number of the then baktun, that of the *katun* to be commemorated, the *tun* year, the number of *uinals*, the day of the *tzolkin* and the day of the *haab*. This initial series was often completed by 'additional series' which specified the lunar month, the phase of the moon and any other elements which might contribute information on the date in question. A highly complicated system, it was later simplified by the decision that only the *katun* number, the *tzolkin* day and its position in the haab would be noted, an abbreviated version which still gave a date which would not recur until 18,980 years or 52 Mayan centuries later!

Counting and numbering were naturally part and parcel of the calendar and here the complex Mayan mind invented a concept of great mathematical and ritual importance, the zero. For them, the vigesimal reckoning of *haab*, for example, was not, as might be thought, from 1 to 20, but from 0 to 19. The Maya divided time into series and considered that the last figure in a series should be left as a space of good omen reserved for the first figure of the next series, a space which would bring it luck. Each number 1 was, in fact, the second day of a new series. Hence the Maya were very early users of this idea of zero (mathematically, an absence of value in a given series), a concept they invented almost 10 centuries before the Arabs received it from Sri Lanka.

Glyphs representing the commemorative date
of an astronomical event found at Palenque.

One of the houses at Joya de Ceren in El Salvador, the 'Pompeii of Central America',
recently cleared of the ash from the neighbouring volcano, Caldera, which smothered the town in the year 600.

Technical innovations in architecture

The inventive genius of the Maya in the field of architecture is all the more remarkable when we consider that, unlike their European or Chinese contemporaries, they lacked certain essential elements such as draught animals, a mastery of hard metals and the wheel. They were obliged to find other solutions and local substitutes for the tools they lacked. Working in human teams (a little like the ancient Egyptians), cleverly using trenches, tree trunks and 'log tracks', the ancient Mayas managed to manipulate and move surprisingly great weights. They specialised in stoneworking, shaping blocks of mostly limestone, sandstone and volcanic trachyte. The early constructions were built from large blocks, cut as best the masons could and sealed with mortar. This imperfect method was soon supplanted by the much more modern technique of concrete formwork. Only the outside face of the stones was now carefully polished and carved. Later, this facing was covered with fine stuccowork painted in bright, predominantly red, colours. The famous Mayan cantilever vault made its appearance towards the early first century BC. Simple in principle and not

considered a true vault, it consisted of a series of corbels, one above the other, projecting successively more and more from a vertical wall, held in place with mortar and capped with a line of flat stones which held them in place like the keystones in a true vault.

The only buildings which have come down to us are those built of stone, the fortresses, temples and various constructions reserved for the aristocracy and the priesthood, notably the 'palaces' - those religious complexes which the Spanish took for royal residences. If the volcano Caldera in El Salvador had not stifled Joya de Ceren (the 'Pompeii of the Mayan world') under a blanket of ash, we would have to guess what simple private dwellings looked like. Because of this catastrophe, we now know that these humble houses were built of adobe. As was supposed before this confirmation, the floors were of beaten clay and the roofs composed of palm fronds attached to a structure of branches. The Mayan man in the street lived like most of the inhabitants of this planet whereas the upper castes, the kings, nobles and priests, lived in sumptuous stone residences, built to resist the passage of time and to proclaim the grandeur of the various city-states.

Mayan æsthetic criteria evolved between the pre-Classic and the post-Classic and these changes in taste have remained recorded in stone. Their weakness for the monumental remains a constant - except in the miniature temples of Tulum - and is certainly attributable to a wish to impress their friends and enemies and to display their technical prowess and wealth. Nothing, in any case, relating to royalty or religion, could be small and mean for the Maya. On this point, it is interesting to note that their palaces and temples were always built on platforms or bases which symbolically raised them above the ground trodden by

Ancient vaulted gallery, called El Pasillo, at Becan in Mexico.

common mortals. These more or less vast pedestals generally took the form of superposed terraces which diminished in size as they rose. In the case of temple-pyramids, such as those of Tikal or Copan for example, these pedestals were solid, rather than hollow, and built with stairs cut into them. Sometimes (but rarely) the base housed a crypt, as at Palenque, intended as a link between the divine world and the humble earth. The steps themselves, leading up to a temple, were considered a sort of initiatory pathway along which the supplicant or officiating priest gradually divested himself of his earthly stains to arrive, purified, in the realm of the gods.

Another typically Mayan characteristic is the verticality of their pyramids. Whereas the other pyramids of Central America tend to occupy space horizontally, the Mayan constructions seem drawn upwards. It may be that this tendency to ascend ever higher was influenced by the omnipresent ocean of trees on their lands, an ocean of green whose waving crests reached 50 metres above the forest floor, but whatever the reason, the impression of verticality is further accentuated by the steep, narrow staircases without

handrails, the high roof ridges of the upper temples, the succession of terraces which seem to taper as they rise skywards and the deliberate lengthening of the masonry blocks.

The temple itself, whether built on a single terrace (at Tulum, Zaculeu, San Andres...) or perched on the summit of a high pyramid (at Tikal, Palenque, Uxmal, Chichen Itza...), is always topped with a large and very heavy roof which invariably posed problems for the architects, obliging them to reinforce the walls. This roof was a highly symbolic feature. It represented the summit of the earthly world and had to magically prevent mere mortals and evil influences from ascending to the upper world. Seen as the ultimate impassable barrier, a real spiritual bolt, it had to be massive and weighty. To alleviate the difficulties this posed, various solutions were adopted. Geometrical holes were pierced along the roof ridges of some temples and semi-pyramidal designs were adopted for others, narrow and very pointed at the top. Much lighter than solid stone but convincingly solid-looking, stucco was employed almost everywhere and, failing all else, to spread the weight of their coverings, inside walls were doubled and tripled.

Structure I at Tazumal (El Salvador) is composed of two superposed pyramidal platforms.

Most of the monuments at Zaculeu in Guatemala, built on square, vertical foundations,
bear witness to the lack of invention which characterises post-Classic architecture.

The Nohoch Mul or Grand Pyramid at Coba in Mexico.
Culminating 120 feet above the ground, it ranks as the highest structure in the Yucatán.

Aerial view of the city of Palenque (Mexico).
Whereas Temple II, the Temple of Inscriptions,
the 'Palace' and the group of the three Temples of the Cross can be distinguished,
we see that most of the site is still covered with forest.

The main square in Tikal (Guatemala) stands surrounded by the ruins of high buildings such as these, here, of the Northern Acropolis.

The classicism of Great Peten and Usumacinta

The name 'Great Peten' refers to a vast architectural area covering a hundred or so sites hidden in the thick tropical forests of northern Guatemala, western Belize and the extreme south of the Mexican Yucatan. Many have not yet been excavated and others certainly remain undiscovered. Great Peten encompasses some huge sites, like Tikal, El Mirador or Rio Azul (all still largely unexplored) and other smaller locations (such as Tayasal, Uaxactun, Yaxja, Nakum, El Zotz, Dos Pilas and Nakbe in Guatemala, Chan Chih, Xunantunich, Lamanaï, Altun Ha, Lubaantun and Caracol in Belize and Calakmul in the Yucatan) which

are often equally interesting. Although each town developed its own culture, Tikal was unquestionably the cultural beacon illuminating the region throughout the entire Classic period with the exception of the 6th century, when Caracol overshadowed its brilliance.

Inhabited between the years 1500 and 900 BC, these different cities did not develop significantly until the Old Classic period and reached their peak during the Modern Classic era between 600 and 800 AD. They share similarities in architectural and decorative styles which are unknown elsewhere in the Mayan lands. The outstandingly delicate workmanship of the pyramid-temples and the stelæ allows us to date their political and historical milestones very precisely. The architectural tendency towards verticality, mentioned above, reached its (literal) height with buildings stretching 70 metres skywards like the Tiger pyramid in El Mirador and Temple IV in Tikal. These constructions, remarkable for their well-balanced and symmetrical proportions, dominate the site with their strong, massive forms. Their bases are constructed from superposed, battered terraces with rounded corners and the central stairway stands out from the plane of the edifice. The temples at the summit, small with massive walls, are coiffed with heavy roof ridges,

Temple II at Tikal is made up of three superposed platforms served by a monumental stairway in one single flight of steps.
On the summit stands a temple topped with a high ridge crest.

higher than the sanctuary itself, supported by a rear wall several metres thick. The facades are often covered with stucco decorated with reliefs and those facing eastwards (in the highly symbolic direction of the rising sun) are always much more richly worked. The architects made extensive use of wooden beams, setting them into the masonry blocks to form door lintels and the upper stiffening of the vaults.

A similar use of wood is also a characteristic feature of the so-called Usumacinta region. This river, a natural frontier between Mexico and Guatemala, has given its name to an architectural style which, covering that of the Chiapas too, is best illustrated in the site called Palenque. Other major ancient cities,

The 'Palace' at Palenque is an imposing building containing several courtyards and a maze of corridors. Its three-storey tower stands 45 feet tall.
The famous crypt under the Temple of Inscriptions at Palenque contains the tomb of King Pakal.
The lid of the sarcophagus is covered with remarkable engravings of the king riding a monster or falling from its maw.

Overall view of the Bonampak Acropolis in Mexico, crowned with several little temples,
and a detail of the lintel of the eastern door to Structure I.

such as Tonina, Bonampak and Yaxchilan in Mexico and Piedras Negras in Guatemala, also contribute to the architectural wealth of this area but Palenque was the first Mayan site discovered in the late 19th century. Of the some 500 buildings counted in the surrounding forest, only 34 have been cleared today. The pyramids, much less pointed than those of the Great Peten, are built with ramp-like staircases leading up to the topmost temple. More spacious than those in Peten, these summit temples are often built of two rooms, the rearmost housing the actual sanctuary. The roof ridge, sometimes built in openwork, is smaller and supported by the partition wall between the two rooms. The buildings of Peten created a style based on

the solid bulks of the architectural forms whereas those of Usumacinta play on the spaces left between the masses. The majestic power of Peten is counterbalanced by the light elegance of Palenque. The cities of Usumacinta were influenced by both, by the massive Peten style and the airy Palenque architecture, and developed their own identity by giving added bulk to the latter and by lessening the vertical tendencies of the former. The arts of painting and sculpture blossomed here more than anywhere else during the Classic period, moving away from the stylized and developing along lines which became very precise and highly lifelike. Carved in stone or painted on the inside walls, the characters grimace and bleed, their features creased with age or swollen with rage. The vertical walls framing the gateways into Yaxchilan and Piedras Negras are sculptured with magnificent reliefs and Bonampak's structure 1 houses one of the finest frescoes in the Mayan world.

The Bonampak site, in the thick of the Usumacinta forest, houses the most complete set of Mayan paintings.
The most interesting cover the walls of Structure 1.

The Motagua baroque

Spreading from eastern Guatemala over into western Honduras, the Motagua river basin was the seat of an original style of architecture which developed between the 5th and the 9th centuries AD. Although falling within the Classic period, the city-states of this area developed a wholly new style of art based on the widening and levelling of constructions, on the employment of an exception number of great monoliths and on a decorative complexity which has led a good number of experts to qualify it as a genuine Mayan

baroque. Quirigua in Guatemala and Copan in Honduras, two rival cities lying only 50 kilometres apart, are perfect illustrations of this tendency. In Copan, the temples, ceremonial platforms and wide tribunes, surrounded by vast esplanades, all offer sweeping vistas. Altars carved with toads, snakes, turtles or crocodiles stand everywhere and magnificent stelæ portray the *halach huinic* standing, as demanded by Mayan custom. Higher than the traditional Mayan versions, these stelæ are decorated with relief sculptures so high as to be almost in the round, a refinement practically unknown elsewhere in the Mayan world. The same must have been the case for Quirigua, but successive depredations have precluded any clear picture of the overall site. It still contains many stelæ, all between 5 and 9 metres high and a giant, named Stela E, which, with its 10.66 metres, ranks as the largest yet found. Quirigua is also famed for its zoomorphs, those stone blocks, 3 to 4 metres long, carved in the shape of fabulous crouching animals, two-headed monsters, giant turtles, serpents, birds or jaguars.

The ball-game court south of the main square in Copán (Honduras)
is one of the largest in Central America, second only to Chichen Itza.

General view of the hieroglyph-inscribed main stairway at Copán. Stela M, standing at its foot, is decorated with a king in a feathered cloak.
One of the zoomorphs (stonecarvings of mythical animals) from Quirigua in Guatemala.

The proliferation of styles in the Yucatan and Campeche

When the Classic period came to a close, the cultural and political centre of the Mayan world soon shifted towards the northern lowlands. From around the year 800 AD, the northern regions of Campeche and the Yucatan, peopled with small settlements since the pre-Classic days, saw great cities develop, flourish and die, each in turn proudly carrying the torch of Mayan identity. This vast area was the theatre of the cultural transition between the Classic and the post-Classic. Flat and much more accessible than the great southern forests, it was the homeland of several peoples, some genuinely Mayan and others from the Mexican tablelands and the Gulf coast, who fought and intermixed with one another. These crosscurrents gave rise to an abundance of cultures and a corresponding wealth of architectural and artistic styles, the best known being, from South to North, those of Rio Bec, the Chenes zone and the Puuc region. The Rio Bec province

includes many sites (many of which have still not been cleared or excavated) scattered in the tropical jungle north of Great Peten in the southern part of the Yucatan. Those which have been partially explored and studied, apart from the various groups of Rio Bec itself, include Chicanna, Becan, Xpujil, Hormiguero and Balamku. All are made up of characteristically long, low buildings, far removed from the usual gigantism of the Classic period. Each facade generally features a wide door created as the gaping maw in a huge mask of the land monster Itzamna, the Mayan god of creation. The monster is represented fullface and his lower jaw forms the raised threshold into the sanctuary. His eyes glare through curved pupils and his lips are drawn back to reveal a row of menacing fangs. This Rio Bec area also boasts astonishing buildings which are generally known as 'palaces' or 'false temples'. Created for some purpose yet undiscovered, these are constructions topped with three little sham pyramid-temples. Perfect miniature replicas, down to the last detail (even fitted with very steep little staircases with steps so small they cannot be climbed!), of the traditional Mayan pyramid-temples, these solid-built little imitations probably had some symbolic function in the rituals of the land.

Northwest of the Rio Bec region, the Chenes province developed its own particular style from the 6th century onwards. It adopted some themes from the former, including the gaping jaws of Itzamna around the entrance doors, but added many new elements, later incorporated into the Puuc style, such as foundation

Structure 1 at the Xpujil site in Mexico, with its three little false temple-pyramids and their dummy stairs,
is a typical example of the Rio Bec style.

The gaping maw of the god Itzamna welcomes visitors at the entrance to Structure II in Chicanna in Mexico.

Partial view of the central square at Becán (Mexico). The site's Mayan name means 'path of the serpent' -
a reference to the protective moat which once surrounded the city.

masses with sloping or stepped sides, engaged colonnettes and columns to divide up the blind parts of the facades, corner masks (often in the effigy of Chac, the Rain god), long and intricate geometrical friezes, lavish lattice-work screens and stylized huts to decorate the facades, high, openwork roof ridges supported by the inner walls of the facade... Decoration became richer to the point of over-abundance and style focused constantly on detail. Many sites are still not cleared and the most accessible today are those of Hochob and Dzibilnocac in the vicinity of Hopelchen. The Chenes style strongly influenced the architecture of several towns in the Puuc region (such as Uxmal) and especially Edzna, a great city-state which is sometimes classified in the Puuc group and sometimes in the Chenes. Although the latter style predominates in most of its buildings, Edzna subsequently freed itself from this cultural imprint, breaking away to create its own artistic personality.

The long road linking Campeche to Chichen Itza follows several sections of the ancient Mayan network of trails connecting Uxmal, Kabah, Labna, Jiuic, Xlabpak, Oxjintok, Xul, Chamultun, Bakna, Itzimte, Sayil, Chichen Itza and others, all cities which reached their peak between the 9th and 11th centuries. The Puuc style is characterized by a simplification of volumes and a carefully calculated balance between sculptured and plain elements. Much more intellectual and abstract than the preceding styles, it produced lengthened buildings, built from juxtapositions of cubes or rectangles, with many doors and - a feature practically never seen before in the Mayan world - columns used to lighten what was considered the overly massive appearance of the facades and allow the openings to be enlarged. The rich ornamentation (sharp quoins, chamfered mouldings, stone mosaics, clear delimitation between different vertical panels, highlighting of vertical planes, pre-eminence of a lavishly worked upper string-course, a wealth of engaged colonnettes and of fullface masks of Itzamna and Chac on the facades...) was no longer merely some æsthetic addition but now very much an architectural element in its own right. The 'palaces' of Kabah (notably the Codz Poop) and of Labna, the so-called Governor's Palace and the Nuns' Quadrilateral in Uxmal and the Red House in Chichen Itza are the most representative examples we have of the Puuc style.

The ruins of Hochob (Mexico) barely emerge from the jungle.
The buildings, such as the main temple pictured here, are covered with outstanding friezes and sculptures in the Chenes style.

In Mexico, the main square at Edzna ('House of Echoes') is overlooked by the five-stepped Great Pyramid.
A stairway of 65 steps leads up to the temple on the summit.

Despite its popular name, the 'Palace' at Sayil in Mexico is a religious building with three superposed steps.
The facade, some 250 feet long, is decorated with the little columns typical of the Puuc style.

The famous arch at Labna (Mexico) and two details of the 'Palace' walls decorated with masks of the god Chac and serpents holding a human head in their mouths.

Group composed of the House of the Turtles, the Great Pyramid and the Dovecot, seen from the summit of the Devin Pyramid at Uxmal in Mexico.
The Devin Pyramid, 117 feet high, is build on an unusual oval base.

General view of the Nuns' Quadrilateral in Uxmal which, despite its name, more probably housed a military academy or a royal school.
The vaulted passages of the Governor's Palace at Uxmal were partially walled at some later period for use as homes.

The Maya-Mexican styles in the eastern regions

From the waning of the Classic period and throughout the entire post-Classic, the general decline of the Mayan city-states in the Yucatan peninsula attracted various groups from central Mexico, notably the Toltecs and the Mixtecs. Several minor styles emerged locally, essentially in the eastern ranges of the

Yucatan and the Quintana Roo, but also in eastern Belize and western Guatemala. Some very quickly attained great importance, the most remarkable being that of the Chichen Itza region. This was an interesting mixture of Mayan and Toltec styles, where the Mexican taste for the monumental and for war combined with the orderly Puuc conception. Here, in Chichen Itza, we encounter some of the finest monuments of the entire Mayan area, creations such as the Caracol, the complex of ballgame courts with the Temple of the Jaguars, the Temple of the Warriors, the Castillo and many others. Structures dedicated to the Wind god, Ehecatl-Quetzalcoatl, gigantic heads of plumed serpents decorating the tops and bottoms of the stairways, serpentiform columns, flat roofs supported by pillars decorated with warriors, altars of skulls, altars supported by telamones and caryatides, *chac-mools*, paintings and sculptures of warriors and priests

The central stairway of the Pyramid of the Masks at Kohunlich (Mexico) is decorated with a double row of giant stucco masks, each around 9 feet high, representing the sun god.

participating in a decapitation, omnipresent representations of felines and eagles... all bear witness to the Mexican influence. Other architectural elements, such as the huge peristyles formed by rows of columns or the replacement of the roof ridge by an alignment of emblems along the edge of the roof, are quite new and testify to the inventiveness of this style.

This was the last flowering of monumental art in the Mayan zone. When Chichen Itza and its successor, Mayapan, began their inexorable decline in the 13th century, other city-states, farther to the east,

attempted to continue the Mayan-Mexican tradition by building ceremonial centres, but these were often on a very reduced scale, dwarfed by the general size of the buildings surrounding them. Striking illustrations of this almost pathetic tendency may be seen in Tancah, Xel Ha and, especially, Tulum, the main fortified town on the Caribbean coast of Quintana Roo. Most of the structures (built from poor-quality masonry) are so small that any human religious activity would have been very difficult if not impossible. No priest could have stood upright in the Temple of Frescoes, famous for its combination of Mayan, Toltec and Mixtec styles. Further south, the sites of Lamanaï and Altun Ha in Belize, of Topoxte, Tayasal, Iximche, Mixco Viejo and Zaculeu in Guatemala and of Tazumal and San Andres in El Salvador enjoyed a brief cultural renaissance when emigrants from Mexico came to settle in these ancient centres, some of which had been inhabited for more than 6 000 years. These incomers interbred with the Mayan locals and produced an enriched dual culture which glowed wanly until the arrival of the Europeans.

Structure A VI, also known as El Castillo, seen from square A I at Xunantunich in Belize.

Once surrounded with fortifications,
the city of Tulum has preserved several of its bastions overlooking the Caribbean.

Three details illustrating the originality of Tulum:
a figure of the 'descending god' or 'diving god' in the little temple of the same name,
paintings and a pillar decorated with a divine mask reminiscent of that of Quetzalcoatl in the Temple of Frescoes.

Although certain areas have still not been cleared from the surrounding jungle, Chichen Itza (Mexico) is undoubtedly the most exceptional
post-Classic architectural site (here the stone throne in the form of a red jaguar with jade eyes in one of the Castillo crypts and one of the heads decorating ▷
the Platform of Jaguars and Eagles) and includes, notably, the largest ball-game court in the Mayan world.

A Cakchiquel lady from Guatemala,
recognizable by the colours and design of her huipil.

Who are the Maya today?

Despite the sharp population drop
caused firstly by the conquest
and the European colonisation and latterly
by the pressure of the modern world and the
mestizos, today's Maya,
some 7,500,000 strong, form the largest Indian
community in America. They are spread over an area
of some 330,000 square kilometres where
28 different official languages are spoken.

Quiché Indian woman from the still rather isolated region of Aguacatan in Guatemala.
The women's costumes worn by the Ixils in the Guatemalan Sierra de Cuchumatanes are among the most colourful in the Mayan world.
This lady is from Nebaj. A Tzotzil lady wearing the traditional headgear or tzute on the principal market at San Cristobal de las Casas in Mexico.

*The women in the Mexican Yucatán have remained faithful to the costumes of their foremothers
and still enjoy a privileged status within their society.*

The Maya from the highlands, less exposed to outside influences, have preserved their customs more than elsewhere (costumes, division of work according to gender, traditional chieftains and priest-healers…). Here we see two Quichés at the Chichicastenango market in Guatemala, an alcalde from San Juan Chamula in Mexico and a Cakchiquel from Solola in Guatemala.

*Colour is an essential element in the everyday symbolism of the Maya
and each ethnic group wears the emblems of its clan. Here we have Tzutuhils carrying water from Lake Atitlan in Guatemala
and a group of Tzeltals from Ocosingo in Mexico.*

A diversity of ethnic groups

Today's Mayan lands cover the Mexican states of Chiapas, northern Campeche, the Yucatan and Quintana Roo, Belize, Guatemala, western El Salvador and Honduras. The Indians now like to speak of their 'Mayan nation', but this name papers over many ethnic cracks. Their various languages are classified into eight principal linguistic families, each subdivided into various groups which themselves include many sub-groups. These great ethno-linguistic groups are very difficult to divide; most of them include ethnic groups which may well be related but are very dissimilar. To avoid the danger of excessive subdivisions, it is perhaps wiser to mention only the main Mayan groups and their numbers. The Chols, numbering around 120,000, live in Mexico, in the mountains of northern Chiapas and in Tabasco, next to the 37,000 Chontals living in the Chontalpa region on the Tabasco coast. The huge Yucatan family includes 840,000 genuine Yucatans, permanently settled on the peninsula and in northern Belize, to whom should be added the shadowy 450 Lacandons from the eastern Chiapas forests, the 2 500 Itzas from around Lake Petén in Guatemala and the 8 500 Mopans from northern Belize. 335,000 Tzeltals and 300,000 Tzotzils live to-gether in the chilly Chiapas mountains. In the east of the state, near the Guatemalan border, 48,000 Tojolabals live in the various highland towns, while, in the south, a scant 6 000 Motozintlecs struggle to survive. The mountains of nouthwest Guatemala provide refuge for many ethnic Mayas, notably the 29,000 Chujs who people the northernmost regions, the 650,000 Mams and the 71,000 Ixils who continue to eke out an existence on the Altos de Cuchumatanes. 910,000 Quichés, 78,000 Tzutuhils and 410,000 Cakchiquels form the most important Mayan concentration in the central Guatemalan tablelands and the surrounding mountains. Further east, we find 280,000 Kekchis and 95,000 Pokomchis. The mountains lying along either side of the border between Guatemala and Honduras are home to 52,000 Chortis. To these complex groups should be added simpler groups such as those living in the Guatemalan highlands, as, for example, the 12,500 Uspantecs and the 38,000 Rabinals with, to the west, the 85,000 Kanjobals, the 33,000 Solomecs and the 18,000 Acatecs and, to the northwest, the 41,000-strong Pokomams, the 31,000 Poptis and the 3 200 Sicapakenses...

Each village community has its own name, its historical references and its own costume. This diversity gives an incredible (if somewhat anarchic) cultural richness which is unfortunately tarnished by great disparities caused by unequal regional development. Thus we find a handful of Lacandons slowly fading into the shadows of the Chiapas forests amid general indifference while 840,000 perfectly organized Quichés rule contentedly over the Guatemalan highlands. Similarly, the Chujs and the Mams, isolated in the far reaches of Guatemala's western mountains, seem to weigh much less than the massive voting power of 850,000 Mexican Yucatans.

The weight of tradition

Despite the lure of the cities, where increasing numbers go to swell the ranks of an ever-exploited proletariat, most Mayans remain peasants who prefer to live in village communities created by the old *reducciones*, those groupings of Indians convented within a village founded by the missionaries during the colonial days. The community centre par excellence is the central square, a distant descendant of the Spanish *zocalo*, invariably shaded by a spreading tree (silk-cotton, kapok, bombax, sapodilla, fig or some other species) considered as the 'navel of the Earth and the Sky' and taken to represent the cosmic tree. When the European colonial administrators and clergy established these village groups, their aim was to force the natives, accustomed to worshipping their gods in the wide open air, to live in the limited space of a village where the only place of worship was the church, the house of the new Christian God who could not be spoken to in the fields like the old, now-defunct gods. Although these 'cultural prisons' would seen to have worked successfully - today's Mayas still live within the spacial limits traced by the Spaniards - the Indians, with their unsuspected powers of assimilation, have nevertheless managed to furnish their prison with the elements of their ancestral world. *Costumbre* altars, for sacrifices and prayers to the ancient divinities, are to be found everywhere, sometimes right next to the church. Christian crosses rub shoulders with anthropomorphic idols. Ancient obituary customs are still practised around the villages, at the four cardinal points where the 'corners of the world' have been planted according to the Mayan conception of the universe.

The last of the Lacandons, a people on the brink of extinction, live in the thick forests of Chiapas. ▷
The boat is often the only means of travel in their swamp world.

Daily chores are many and difficult in the Guatemalan Altos. Men and women (as this Quiché from Nahuala and this Ixil lady from Nebaj)
share the heavy work of transporting wood to keep the home fires burning. Harsh living conditions take their toll.
Despite appearances, neither this Pokomam nor this Tzutuhil from Guatemala has reached fifty!

*In the Mayan world, the womenfolk are the guardians of tradition and one of their major responsibilities is to educate the children in the 'Mayan path',
teaching them the ancestral language and handing down customs. Here we see Yucatecs from Tihosuco and Tzotzils from Zinacantan (Mexico).*

The community may be seen as a group, but the family is still the basic unit in Mayan society. Each has a head who rules over all the members and whose responsibility it is to see that the 'blood' of the ancestors is respected; in other words, to ensure that the tradition of lineage is upheld. These heads of family elect councillors who are placed under the authority of the town's chief administrative and judicial officer, the *alcalde*. The councillors take decisions on everything affecting community life, calling up participants for collective work, organizing festivities, negotiating with the administrative authorities... They proudly wear their badges of office, the ceremonial stick symbolizing judicial and executive power, the necklace of silver coins, the wide belt strapped round their waist and, for the most important among them, the lavishly decorated hat. The Guatemalan *sajorins* and the Yucatan *h'mens* occupy similar functions, the latter being more akin to shamans, however, invested with supernatural powers, practising divination and traditional medicine and sometimes feared by the population. Another important institution is the *cofradrias* or brotherhoods, encouraged by the Spanish from the very outset of the colonisation with the aim of teaching

the Indians to worship saints. These brotherhoods own land and livestock and long served as buffers between the colonial state, to whom they paid taxes in the name of the community, and the Indians, whose pagan religious practices they protected with a cloak of secrecy. The rôle of the brotherhoods suddenly grew in the 19th century when the missionary orders were expropriated and driven out by the new liberal rulers. The brotherhoods each have a sanctuary-house, where the pagan-Christian 'saint' lives, and act as spiritual governments for their communities, laying down the law with regard to community traditions.

Although the main lines of Mayan tradition are thus largely constant (corn, for example, in its three forms - yellow, white and black - is still honoured everywhere as a divine blessing), the same is certainly not true for everyday customs, affected both by lineage and locality. Because the Mayan lands spread from the highlands of the Mexican Chiapas and Guatemala to the lowlands of the Yucatan, Belize, Honduras and El Salvador, clothes and houses are necessarily very different. The warm Indian costume of the highlands has survived better than its cool counterpart in the warm lowlands, more easily replaced by western clothes. Dwellings in the cool tablelands are generally built of adobe bricks with a heavy tile roof while those of the subtropical flatlands are often long oblong huts, partitioned by latticed wooden screens, or rectangular or square houses constructed on the wattle and daub principle.

A group of peasant women offering their products on the little daily village market.
Totonicapan in Guatemala.

Claims still unsettled

On the morning of the 1st of January 1994, learning that an armed commando of the EZLN (Zapatist National Liberation Army) had occupied the towns of the Chiapas the night before to cries of 'Ya basta!' (We've had enough!), the world suddenly discovered that there was a Mayan problem. This date coincided with the coming into force of the North American Free Trade Agreement, and had thus been deliberately chosen to denounce the trade agreements Mexico had signed with the United States and Canada while the Maya were struggling to survive.

The rebels, mostly pure Indians led by a mysterious 'subcommander Marcos', sought to crack the politically correct image of the country given by the P.R.I. (Institutional Revolutionary Party) in power at the time, demanding their share of the freedom and equality written into the Mexican constitution. Under pressure from the North American nations and the international financial powers, who took a very dim view of this unknown threat to the new economic order of the region, the government responded brutally by sending in the army, convinced that the matter would be settled within a few days.

They were badly mistaken. Despite heavy repression, the EZLN pursued its action and the election of a new president, Ernesto Zedillo, in no way changed things. Several districts of the Chiapas proclaimed their separatist status, declaring home rule. Little has changed since, except that the EZLN is now the FZLN, no longer an Army but now a Front. Hundreds of civilians have been killed and the Mexican government continues its policy of repression.

Those who were surprised by this sudden flare-up of violence in a region so popular with tourists should bear in mind that this was neither the first nor, certainly, the last rebellion on Mayan territory. The great

Ladies from the Tzutuhil people in Guatemala wear this astonishing headgear made up of a long ribbon of red cloth,
attached at one end to a lock of hair and then wound round the head and held in place with a richly embroidered band.

uprisings of the late 17th and 18th centuries (notably in 1692 and again in 1712 in the Chiapas and in 1761 in the Yucatan) were simply the most publicised of a long series of insurrectional movements which all tended towards the same aim of obtaining, if not independence, at least official recognition of the Mayan identity.

The Aztec *caciques* [2] may have been pressed into the colonial mould by accepting administrative duties or European titles, but most of the Mayan chiefs scorned or ignored these inducements. Whenever foreign pressure became too strong, the pot boiled over and the Mayan capacity for violence and sudden rebellion

was equalled only by their Indian patience. The Indians have remained unheard in certain countries simply because the Maya are too few and their voice too weak or because of the democratic gag tied tight by certain régimes. In Belize, the English colonial system more or less subordinated the Indians to the blacks, forcing them to seek support from the whites and the *mestizos* and, thus, to hide many of their demands. In El Salvador and Honduras, where they represent respectively only 6.7% and 9% of the population, they have been literally engulfed by successive governments. It was not until Carlos Roberto Reina became president of Honduras in 1993 and Calderon Sol was elected in El Salvador in 1994 that some interest began to be shown in the Mayan minority. Guatemala, with its 54% Mayan contingent, is quite another case. The Indian voice should have rung louder here than elsewhere, yet this is where it has been most stifled for centuries past. Even in the agreement of December 29th 1996, which put an end to 36 years of civil war, the Maya remained at the bottom of the pile, the forgotten nation within a nation.

History marches on regardless. The rulers of the various Central American lands would do well to heed the Mayan voice, even if only to avoid the reactions of a desperate nation with nothing left to lose...

[2] Native Indian chief in an area dominated by Spanish culture

This Mam from the Cuchumatanes in Guatemala is a highly respected chieftain among his own people.
He is wearing the traditional Mayan red headscarf and the colours of his clan on the collar of his jacket.

Summing-up

They call it the 'dark legend', the story of how the Spanish conquered America and exacted their reward. This sombre name took root in the mid 16th century, when Italy, followed by Flanders and Germany and soon after by the rest of Europe, accused the Spanish Crown, its administration, its soldiers and its clergy of having committed a veritable genocide with regard to the Indian populations. These attacks had ulterior motives, of course; the adversaries of Spain were jealous of her having been the first to beach on the American continent and, thereby, of having derived an income so substantial as to enable her to build, in the words of the Holy Roman Emperor Charles V, a gigantic empire on which 'the sun never set'. Yet whatever the motives, Spanish responsibility is practically unalleviated as regards the subsequent misfortunes of the Amerindians, whether the decimation caused by forced labour or the ravages of European diseases. Estimated at almost 100 million by Berkeley (considerably lower by other researchers) when the Europeans disembarked, the overall Indian population on the American continent, fragmented into some 1 400 peoples speaking 2 600 languages, fell to 25 million by the closing years of the 16th century. According to the latest research, 10 million of these people lived in what is now northern Mexico, another 30 million in the centre and south and a further 11 million in the rest of Central America. In less than a century, the local population fell by 70 to 75% on average!

This said, the Amerindians were far from being the 'noble savages', imagined by Rousseau, living pure and blameless lives. Most were warriors who waged merciless war with one another and practised a bloodthirsty religion where ritual sacrifices and anthropophagy were the rule. The arrival of the Europeans was a welcome liberation for many peoples. Western civilization introduced new medicines, hygiene, administration... Yet the trauma of the brutal white invasion, although five centuries old, has never healed; today's Indian communities still cannot understand why, in the name of God and the kings of Europe, their civilizations were destroyed to be replaced by a system equally violent and unjust.

Mesoamerican history has been written ever since (in words and deeds) by the whites or *mestizos*, through revolutions and through North American influences. The only future for the subcontinent lies in a reconciliation between its tumultuous past and its equally turbulent present. This implies recognition of the Indian identity and acceptance of the fact that cohabitation of all four communities is an enrichment rather than an obstacle for the future.

When Central America is at last left in charge of its own destiny and proud of its unique diversity, then it will become what it should be - the jewel of the American continent.

Three children from the Tarahumara people in front of the local church in Cusarare (Mexico).
Do these girls incarnate hope for the Indians of Central America?

Design and graphics
BOWER
3 place aux Huiles - 13001 Marseilles, France

Photocomposition, photoengraving and cartography
PLEIN FORMAT
72 boulevard Notre-Dame - 13006 Marseilles, France

Printing
EGEDSA
Rois de Corella, 12-16, Nave 1
08205 Sabadell / Barcelone, Spain

© 1999 VILO
25 rue Ginoux - 75015 Paris, France

Printed edition september 1999
Legal inscription october 1999
ISBN : 2 719 10454-X